COUNTRY ON ICE

COUNTRY
O·N ✦ I·C·E
DOUG BEARDSLEY

POLESTAR PRESS
WINLAW BC

Published by
Polestar Press Ltd., R.R. 1, Winlaw, B.C., V0G 2J0 604-226-7670

Canadian Cataloguing in Publication Data
Beardsley, Doug - 1941
Country on ice
Bibliography
ISBN 0-919591-22-1
I. Hockey - Canada   II. Hockey - physical aspects - Canada
III. Hockey - Canada - History
GV848.4.C3B43 1987   796.9'62'0971   C87-091486-3

Country On Ice was designed and produced by Polestar Press in
Winlaw, B.C., and printed by Hemlock Printers in Vancouver.

Contents

Sports is just a paradigm of life, right? Otherwise, who'd care a goddamn thing about it?

— Richard Ford, *The Sportswriter*

Civilization begins at the moment sport begins.

— Nikos Kazantzakis, *Report to Greco*

Acknowledgements

I've wanted to write this book for 30 years and didn't know it — a book that encompassed the boyhood experience of growing up with the game in Canada, a book that made all our histories *the* history of the country. Michael Gregson encouraged me to do so at the outset.

I'd never have done it were it not for Julian Ross, who approached me first as publisher, then editor, and finally, friend. Often he was all three at once in his attempts to encourage, inspire, and cajole me on to greater heights — or initially any height at all.

To Stephanie Judy I extend my deepest thanks. Her paragraph-by-paragraph comments and sense of overall structure created a book from a manuscript.

To Irving Layton I can only add my thanks: our numerous talks on the game were always an enriching and insightful experience for me.

Special thanks are also due my mother and my brother, whose remembrance of the early years were both detailed and vivid. And to my nephews Anthony and Christopher, who gave of their time and hockey experiences in the early development of the book.

To Colleen Donnelly and Diana Rutherford, my sincere thanks for their expert typing of the manuscript through to the final stage.

Thanks are also due to the people who appear in the pages of *Country On Ice*: Claudia Thompson, Donald Braden, Claire

Johnson, Al Purdy, Becky Smith, Mike Doyle, Winston Jackson, Monsuerrat Gonzalez, Joyce Gutensohn, David Moore, Katherine Chapman, Brenda Herbison, and Bart Nawinski. All shared both their time and their memories of the game we love.

I read hundreds of books, articles, and newspaper columns in the writing of this work, but in the end I took little from them. What I drew on most often were my own experiences, and my own thoughts and feelings about what is good and not-so-good about our national game.

Doug Beardsley
Montreal — Vancouver Island, September 1987

Photo Credits

An anecdote that best exemplifies the natural toughness of the game was told by Trent Frayne in a March 1987 newspaper obituary on Red Dutton. Frayne recalled the time in the Montreal Forum when the referee forgot the puck at the start of the game. There was a short delay while the powers-that-be sought a puck at the timekeeper's bench. Legend has it that Dutton, irritated by the delay, skated up to the referee and snarled: ''Never mind the damn puck. Let's start the game!''

*In memory of John Atkinson (1941 - 1984), shinny master,
the best hockey player who never put on skates.*

Playing the Parlour Game

I remember the morning my grandfather appeared in the kitchen doorway asking for adhesive tape to bandage his bruised knuckles. He wound the thick white tape like surgical gauze over each knuckle on both hands, complaining of the slashing he'd received at the hands of my older brother. Even at the age of two I detected the mock horror in his voice and saw the hint of a smile on his face.

Both Grandfather and my father were hockey fans. Every Saturday after dinner they gathered round the large Marconi radio standing on the floor like a wooden juke-box between the living-room and dining-room of our home.

But the ''real'' game was played on the floor of a tiny alcove in my family's duplex. The six-inch hockey sticks were whittled from carefully chosen twigs. The ice: a red carpet. The rink: an entire set of *Encyclopedia Britannica* laid flat, spines becoming the boards. The puck: a black checker. The room was closed on three sides; a door led off one end to the basement. Whenever a game was in progress and my mother had to get to the cellar for food she'd say, ''Sorry,'' and the game halted momentarily to let her pass. If the score was tied,

15

however, or the game a close one, someone reminded Mother of the white rat that had once been seen at the foot of the stairs, and mentioned that we'd heard odd rustlings, some gnawing perhaps? We wondered aloud if it might be the rat, on the stairs again? Waiting? This strategy, employed by both Grandfather and my brother, never failed to keep the game going during the most tense moments.

Grandfather was retired from the Northern Electric Company and played "hockey" whenever he came to visit us from the other side of the duplex. He had spent much of his life making the gold-leaf edge and filigree on the wooden telephone boxes common in Montreal by the 1940s. It was this same delicate touch he employed when he made the small, durable nets that took such a beating from all the close-in action during a game. The nets were a heavy woven fabric stretched over tiny goalposts; the hard cardboard crossbars were held together with Northern Electric black tape.

My grandfather and my older brother got down on their knees side by side and hacked away at the checker until I heard my grandfather howl and my brother shout, "He shoots! He scores!" Mother occasionally hid the puck to slow the pace of the game and to give my grandfather a sporting chance. Then a marble was quickly brought into play, making slap-shots a hazard, not only to my grandfather's knuckles but also to the china cabinet in the hallway and the increasingly scuffed oriental rug.

Grandfather always dressed formally; even when he went for a walk it looked as if he was going out to dine — crisp white shirt, tie, grey suit and matching vest. When he played the parlour game, this was the outfit he wore, minus the suit jacket. Hockey has always had a high degree of formality and elegance for me, and I've no doubt my feeling comes from early memories of my fastidious grandfather on his aging knees whacking at that black checker. The loop of his solid gold watch-chain occasionally acted as an impediment — or defence-man's check — in his drive toward my brother's net.

Grandfather had reach, my brother agility, and scores were low because of this delicate natural balance. Mother was referee-in-chief. She had an intuitive time-piece that seemed to know the precise moment when Grandfather had taken enough punishment. One thing was certain: when my grandfather stood up the game was over, for he surely wasn't going to be able to get down on his knees again that day. Yet his love for children — in particular for my brother and me — and the pleasure he received from playing the parlour game, meant that he was available both mornings and afternoons during the week. My weekends were spent with my parents, but, as my father was off working during the week, often not returning home 'til after I'd gone to bed, Grandfather had free rein in our house five days out of seven. He came over whenever he felt the urge to see us and play the game, though he was equally as interested in making and maintaining the nets and sticks, a task that provided him with a good winter hobby.

When I was older I too challenged Grandfather but seldom played the parlour game with my brother. He had grown too old for pretend games and had gone on to the real thing out on the street. By the time I was six my grandfather was too old for anything but the occasional short walk. And we had moved up in the world, from that Montreal duplex in the cosmopolitan area of Snowdon to a semi-detached in an exclusive suburb on the other side of Mount Royal.

But that first memory of seeing hockey played on the alcove floor never left me. The parlour game was my first encounter with the world of the imagination. I was hooked.

As a child I could not know that my whole approach to life was being determined by my fascination for this make-believe game. It was only much later, when I was an adult and long past my playing days, that I realized the full effect of ''playing the parlour game.'' I was not interested in reality; something that stood for the game of hockey was more attractive to me than the real thing.

The Sound of the Game

*Hello Canada, and hockey fans in the United States and New-
foundland. The score at the end of the first period is ....*

— Foster Hewitt

The game begins in the ear, inside the head. The game that
you create in your head is often superior to "the real thing"
and far better than the one-dimensional game we see on TV.
For when we hear the game we become part of the game,
we play it. You can *feel* yourself going over the blueline with
Gretzky and Kurri, *you* are racing in from the slot. The great
voices of hockey give one this feeling. They are our ears and
eyes. They do not wear helmets.

How old were we when we first heard the nasal, rasping
voice of Foster Hewitt's "He shoots! He scores!" coming at
us over the airwaves? If "playing the parlour game" was my
invitation to the imaginative world, the game that Foster
Hewitt "created" convinced me that the world of the imagination was where I wished to be. To steal a famous baseball
announcer's axiom: Nothing happened until he said so.

A child's imagination is as wide and open as the world of
which he is so innocent. Having seen an NHL or amateur

game, or dozens of street and corner-rink contests, it is easy for a youngster to imagine a great save by Hall, Plante, Sawchuk, to see Gretzky or Esposito flying over the line. Being able to visualize the game as broadcast, it is a short imaginative leap to being out there on the ice as one of the players, as the hero you always dreamed you'd be. As Ken Dryden wrote in *The Game*: "Foster Hewitt could make us them."

How many of "us" have dreamed we were "the Rocket," the great Beliveau (the personification of Hemingway's "grace under pressure"), the famed Gordie Howe, Bobby Hull, the legendary Orr, "the Flower" before his demise. As young boys we became these men, swooping in on net to let go a drive "right-on." The hockey broadcast on Saturday nights was merely the raw material for the game that was churning inside our heads. The broadcasters were concrete poets dealing in word pictures. Yet everything was in detail, like a good short story.

Millions of Canadians listened to Saturday Night Hockey. We were brought together by Foster Hewitt's measured tones describing a game that was — and still is — one of the great unifying symbols of our country, along with our vast waterways, our railroads and highways, the CFL at Grey Cup time and the CBC. Canadians from all walks of life listened to the game in their living-rooms, kitchens, or basements. Sitting around the fire having supper or doing the dishes. On a farm. In a tiny fishing village. In one of the few big cities in our giant land. No other game has been such a force in bringing our country together. A Canadian boy's dreams were nurtured by Foster Hewitt, for the game we visualized is an essential, fundamental Canadian vision; it is shared: for generations it was a basic part of growing up in Canada.

Those who played the game at a young age carried the

imaginary game with them at all times, especially on Saturday nights after listening to Foster Hewitt. My older brother, David, a natural skater and wonderful hockey player, remembers: ''You carried the puck; when they went in you went in; when someone took a fierce check you felt it. You carved your way down the ice.

''The imaginative grew, became sharper and clearer: 'Should I go into the corner or stay out in front of the net? Should we pinch, or do we move in?' You accelerated so you could anticipate the play. Your mental, imaginative vocabulary was vast. You were well-informed and you put your knowledge to work. You played well, always. You went to sleep knowing you'd made the NHL.''

Dave was a Leaf fan at a very early age because of Hewitt's broadcasts and later because of the inspirational play of Ted ''Teeder'' Kennedy. ''I remember building a crystal set and rubbing that little brush of the crystal, moving it 'til the right contact was made and Foster Hewitt's voice was loud and clear...for a minute or so. I wasn't satisfied with what I received over the crystal set *until* I got the hockey game and then and only then was the crystal set working. I'd get FDR or Winston Churchill making a major speech but nothing counted until I got the game. I made my own domain within comfortable boundaries. For certain misbehaviours, you'd be disciplined to your room. To hockey! However, in terms of the real world, it was an extremely chauvinistic world, and *very* insular.''

Foster Hewitt often made the game more exciting than it was. Indeed, it was said by some that he ''invented'' hockey in the minds of young Canadians. Asked once why he liked the game so much Hewitt replied: ''It represents the very best of Canadians .... The men in it have the ability to give and take.''

Unlike the posturing, pretentious Howard Cosells of our

time who operate on the assumption that a second of silence is a criminal offence, Hewitt used the dramatic pause to increase the tension of the game. It was one of his best broadcasting techniques. He needed no ex-hockey player at his side posing as a colour-man; he did it all.

Who will ever forget the voice of Foster Hewitt cracking with emotion as he described Paul Henderson's series-winning goal against the Soviets in Moscow? September 28, 1972. Ten million Canadians watched Neil Armstrong take one small step for mankind on the moon. Twelve million Canadians heard Henderson's goal. Canadians who remember where they were and what they were doing when John F. Kennedy was assassinated in Dallas nine years earlier also remember what they were doing on the day when there were 34 seconds left to play and "He shoots! He scores!"

Foster Hewitt was not the first voice of hockey. Mr Norman Albert broadcast the final period of a game between Midland and North Toronto in February 1923. Less than a month later, an equally forgotten hockey pioneer by the name of LD "Pete" Parker broadcast the first full play-by-play of a playoff game between the Edmonton Eskimos (yes, that's right) and the Regina Caps, the final game for the championship of the WCPHL, the Western Canada Professional Hockey League. (Even in the world of sports Canadians have paid little attention to their pioneers. Perhaps because the game was only broadcast in Regina, the mysterious Mr Parker never received the recognition he deserves.) Hewitt's first play-by-play followed approximately a week later in Toronto; another decade and his was the first voice heard across the nation.

In the two solitudes that comprised the Quebec I grew up in during the '40s and '50s, English Quebecers were weaned on the dulcet tones of Doug Smith, a little-remembered CBC sportscaster who died of cancer several years ago.

Just as the gondola atop Maple Leaf Gardens in Toronto was Foster Hewitt's home, the catwalk of the Montreal Forum was the personal perch for a kid from Cape Breton named Danny Gallivan for over 30 years.

It was Gallivan, the voice of the Montreal Canadiens, who provided us with an imaginative diction and syntax worthy of the game. The game that Gallivan broadcast was not only better than the one being played, it was even more exciting than the one we could "see" in our heads. Danny Gallivan was our first aural poet of the airwaves, creating a weekly one-hour epic that made him the Homer of hockey:

> Duff having difficulty against Dennis Hull they joust each other rather vigourously Reay going with the big guns, Pilote, Nesterenko, Mohns, Chicago every man up Mikita over the line with BOBBY HULL ...

> OOOOhh, and Hull grazes the goalpost on the far side with a CANNONADING SHOT the players race after it, Cournoyer FEEDING IT to the other side Lemaire fails to negotiate contact with the puck now he finds an opening and shoots it down the ice right on target ...

> The Hawks regrouping behind their own line coming out over centre Beliveau STEALS the puck, takes a shot right on the short side and Hall was there to stymie him with a scintillating save Cournoyer now CUTTING IN on goal, trying to get

right IN FRONT   ANOTHER SHOT   the Canadiens
really firing the puck around with authority
Lemaire WINDS UP, Beliveau takes a poke at it
COURNOYER A REAL SPINNERAMA   THEY
BANG AWAY AT IT, THEY BANG IT IN!   and
the Montreal Forum crowd goes crazy!

The intonation of Gallivan's splendid voice, the rise and
fall of his modulations, as inevitable as the ocean's roar, his
tones an octave or two apart, are impossible to reproduce on
paper. Although English-Canadian, Gallivan's Irish ancestry
gave his broadcasts a great sense of excitement and Gallic
urgency that typified the Flying Frenchmen of Montreal.
Gallivan was like a lead opera singer, his tenor voice roaring
above the Forum crowd. In French broadcasting, only Rene
Lecavelier was able to match Danny Gallivan in intensity of
feeling and pure passion. We still carry the echoing voices of
Hewitt and Gallivan out onto the street. Youngsters today
who listen to Vancouver's Jim Robson do the same.

The voices of hockey also appear on the page. Sportswriters have a more difficult time than broadcasters because
they must bring the game alive after the fact. There are only a
few good sportswriters in Canada. The *Globe and Mail* has
cornered some of the best. We have no one the likes of FRC
James, the Trinidadian on cricket, or Neville Cardus on the
same game, or the contemporary American baseball writers
Roger Angell and Thomas Boswell, and no baseball book I
have read matches the one written by the great Japanese
slugger Sadaharu Oh. Aside from Ken Dryden's excellent
The Game, no one has written a major work about hockey, and
to date Roy MacGregor has produced the only novel of note on

25

the subject. It seems we don't take the game seriously away from the ice. If someone is crazy enough to do so, we feel embarrassed by such high-seriousness and usually ship him off to sportsland Siberia. The *Globe and Mail's* Allen Abel is the most current example of this. In recent times, Abel, one of our best sports columnists of the past decade, has been illuminating us with his occasional reports from China.

In Montreal, "Red" Fisher is one who brings a perceptive eye and detailed knowledge to readers. In Quebec, the late Ghyslain Luneau was Abel's rival for the *Journal de Montreal*, the self-billed No. 1 French daily in North America. In French-Canada, a sportswriter like Luneau is as much a star as the players he writes about.

It is a damp and foggy Saturday evening in November 1952. There is no snow on the ground though the boards are up in anticipation in all the city parks. Several dozen kids have cycled down to the Modelelectric Hardware Store, converging on the huge-panelled glass windows as if drawn by some mysterious magnet or evil eye. We lean forward on our icicle-like handlebars, chewing on our stolen chocolate bars. Is it the fog or the evening air or the fogginess of the wavering images through the steamed-up window that gives us a collective squint? Many of us are 11-year-olds who try to act nonchalant and think we are aware of what we are seeing. It is Hockey Night in Canada. On television. But we are not sure if what it "teles" us is what we want to see.

The set is huge, a giant brown box of a thing, the picture tube as big as a bookcase. We are told what we are seeing is taking place *at the same time* 10 miles away, downtown in the Montreal Forum. We know this is so, we believe what we are *told* by the white-shirted salesman, and we bike away to our homes in deep silence accepting it, but we are skeptical and uncertain of what we have *seen*. To this day we remain so. At age 11 we understood not only that we had witnessed history in the making but that our lives had been irrevocably altered.

So was the game. At first it was not so noticeable. We were carried away by the technological magic, as we are now with word processors. But it was not long before the game was broken up by an increasing number of commercial pauses or time-outs that do little but irritate — or at least bore — the at-home audience. In the arena, the natural tempo of the game is being tampered with, changed, almost destroyed.

If a well-played hockey game is a work of art, the art is being interrupted from outside itself for commercial reasons. On ice there is a lessening of tension as a result, and the players are irritated, not to mention the fans. Players don't even fake it anymore; they simply stand around while the referee stares at the little white light that tells him the commercial is still on and when to blow his whistle, drop the puck.

Television is a one-dimensional medium. There is no overview, few intimacies, no time for reflection, no desire to explore anything in depth. Stop-action replays and videos have eroded the imaginative and human aspect of the game. You see a picture chosen by someone else. A single picture is all you see and you react to it or you don't. We live in such an impatient age so eager for instant self-gratification via the new technology that nowadays we can put a hockey game in superspeed and reduce it to a matter of a few minutes or less. Some hockey viewers have video collections of several hundred ''best'' games, a stockpile that would take a lifetime to view. In an American magazine, one south-of-the-border ''fan'' described how he watches all the hockey games in superspeed

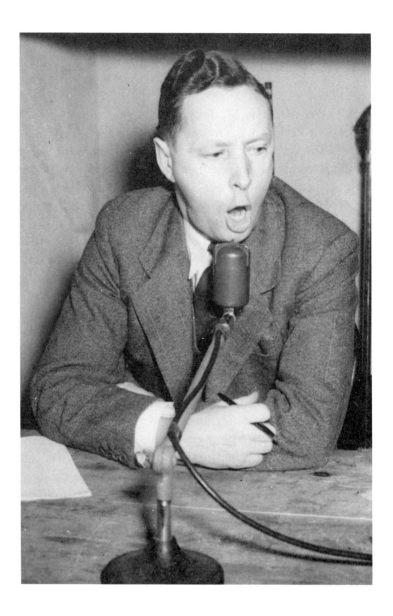

until he sees the sticks being raised in the air (no guarantee of a goal these days!) and then he goes back and watches *only* the goal. The new technology now makes it possible for him to "see" an entire hockey game in ten or twelve minutes. But what is he "seeing"? Does it have anything to do with hockey?

What this fan is missing most of all is the poetry, the subtle ebb and flow of the game, its fluidity, range, and patterns. We have come a long way from the world of the imagination created by Foster Hewitt and Danny Gallivan.

My Country
Is Not a Country...

Mon pays, ce n'est pas un pays, c'est l'hiver.
— **Gilles Vigneault**

*Place is an American idea; place is where people interact...
space is more a Canadian sense. The Group of Seven paintings,
no people in them. Baseball is all about place, home and so on.
Hockey is about space ....*

— **George Bowering**

If the truth be known, we delight in winter. In the season in
which bears hibernate, and death is everywhere, Canadians
come alive. We celebrate Vivaldi's fourth season "trembling
frozen in black frost," skating "in the icy blast of a bitter
wind...with teeth chattering because of the excessive cold,"
and feeling "all the winds at war." In the language of the verse
that accompanies Vivaldi's *Four Seasons*: "This is winter,
but such that it brings joy."

Winter is vitality and energy to us; to come through is an
exhilarating experience. Both hockey and shinny are natural

31

winter ways to use that energy. We complain about it all the time but we love the challenge of winter.

As boys, it often seemed to us that the coming of winter had but one purpose: hockey. Even Christmas meant only one thing: hockey presents. A couple of sticks with ribbons on them standing by the tree. The old puck-in-the-stocking trick (heavy *and* it takes up a lot of room). Among wrapped boxes that revealed father's new shirt or a nightgown for mother there were sure to be hockey socks or gauntlets; there might be long underwear that would be perfect for shinny. And, occasionally, that treasure of treasures, a new Canadiens or Leafs sweater.

Only small pockets of Canada stitched onto the central fabric of our country escape winter. For the rest of us it's four months or more of bone-chilling temperatures, blasting winds, slippery streets and sidewalks of verglas that are as good as skating rinks, warm clothing, mitts and gauntlets heated on radiators, stuck cars, shovelling, and heavy boots that give good traction and stop hard shots without pain. My country is not a country, it's the winter; it's hockey.

I still vividly recall hurrying through my homework after supper so I could meet my friends at the corner precisely at 8:00 p.m. Bundled up against the freezing night, our mother's cold cream covering forehead, lips, nose and cheeks, we made our way over the crunching snow, flight boots kicking through huge drifts that threatened to engulf us. Suddenly, through the swirling snow, we saw our goal: the first arrivals had turned on the string of overhead lights above the rink. The lights swung in the wind like a necklace of beads on a beautiful woman. The ice beckoned, drawing us nearer and nearer like a great white magnet. Our pace quickened, anticipation warmed our blood.

After an hour or two of hard all-out play, we left the rink, our passion satiated 'til the next time. We talked ourselves home, full of heated satisfaction as we remembered and joked about the best moments on ice, reliving the game aloud over and over, shutting out the icy blackness that surrounded us, forgetting the aches and pains we'd willingly received and overcome, remembering only a game of exhilarating grace and beauty.

How many hot dogs, hot chocolates and May Wests did we devour during those precious winter seasons? In hundreds of small towns throughout this country on ice, the local hockey rink is still the centre of the community. It is the place you still hurry to get to — hurry through dinner, through chores, through homework, through the frozen night. It is the place where you can be seen and see everyone you wish. It is the place where relationships are made, hardened, or broken, where the community finds a full expression of its nature. ''The main gathering point in small-town Saskatchewan is still the rink,'' said former Prince Albert coach Terry Simpson. ''In summer it's hustle and bustle and hard work but in winter, because of the climate, hockey has a bonding effect.''

My dentist, Dr Donald Braden, recalls what the game meant on the Prairies in the 1940s and early '50s: ''In Camrose, Alberta, a boy's whole life was hockey. Whether you played for the senior team, the town juvenile team, your school team, or just played pick-up games on the pond, nothing else mattered. The game meant everything. It was the only entertainment in town, the only way up out of mediocrity. Later on, hockey had some competition — a change of movies at the local theatre twice a week — but it was a rare kid who went to the movies more than once a month. Who could afford it? Hockey was the only game in town. I remember when my father bought me a pair of bob skates made of aluminum, two runners in the front and two on the back tied to the overshoes with straps.''

This is not far removed from the crude metalrunners which the Royal Canadian Rifles, an Imperial unit of Her Majesty's, attached to a wooden base on their boots on a bitterly cold Christmas Day in 1855. Using field hockey sticks and a lacrosse ball, they cleared snow from the ice and, near present-day Kingston, laid claim to the title of the founding fathers of hockey.

Starting from bob skates and crude metalrunners, boys from places like Trail, Flin Flon, Smiths Falls, and Glace Bay grew in a geographical space where the pioneer spirit and the need for survival were paramount. The speed, excitement, and danger inherent in the game may be juxtaposed with Canadians giving their all in order to come through a typical Canadian winter. We have learned how to survive as a people, as a country on ice, able to bear the great weight of cold. We think we can overcome it but, in fact, to endure it is our goal. Jim Fanning, head of the Montreal Expos baseball farm system, claims ''there is a certain inner toughness of Canadian kids ... I don't know if it's because they start off playing hockey or because they grow up in a more severe climate, but they won't back down for anything.''

Braden remembers his years in senior hockey in Camrose when ''we thought little of driving 26 miles in a coal truck with a canvas top to play a game. The temperature was often 30 below Fahrenheit. All the guys would be huddled in the back. But we knew it mattered. Hockey was a noble game. For a boy to do well in school and on the rink was excellent.''

Hockey may warm the blood but it is also a cold game, played in the bleakness of winter in often severe conditions. When Dan Hodgson of the junior champion Prince Albert Raiders

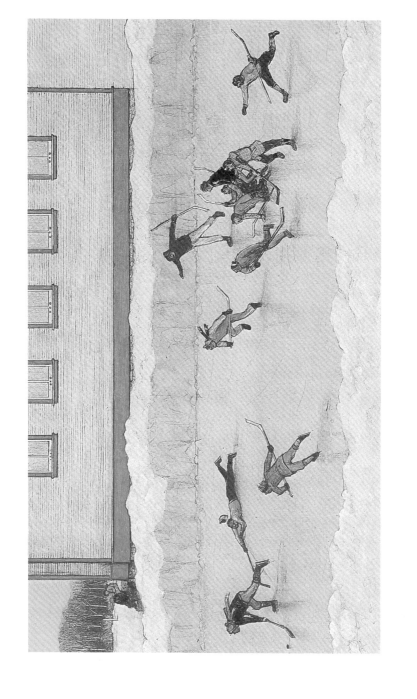

was drafted by the then-lowly Toronto Maple Leafs he said: "I'd really like to play in Toronto ... it's so warm down there. I want to get out of the cold."

For some, the hockey rink was the only place where a Canadian youngster had a chance at a meaningful career, a career in which he could acquire a sense of self-confidence and make money. On the ice he could carve out his own life and create his own history. Former Soviet coach Tarasov considers his Russian players and concludes, "We do not have the spirit to draw on that these Canadians do." They have "a light that cannot be put out ... You defeat them sometimes, but you discourage them never."

Hockey has created our history, too. It is not possible to imagine what Canadian life would be like without hockey. Even the most jaded fans know that the game means something more than the pure pleasure of identifying with their favourite athlete or team. When they are there, in the Montreal Forum or Maple Leaf Gardens or the Northlands Coliseum for a few hours each week, they enter into a mythical world beyond their day-to-day reality. Hockey began here, in the mythic. As a result, what can be said mythically about the game applies to us, our culture, and our country.

Poet and professor Mike Doyle, a native of New Zealand, says that what most attracts him as an outsider to hockey is that the game "has its own folklore ... it couldn't have come from anywhere else but Canada." Doyle is intrigued by the elaborate dressing for the game and its counterpart of dressing for the Canadian climate.

Hockey is an allegory of our life in Canada as Canadians and of our role in society and our role in the world. We are in between the world's superpowers, skating in circles at centre ice. Yet this fact need not lead us to the defeatist attitude that at times dominates the Canadian will. It can also be a clarion call to play the game with the reckless abandon of the crazy Canuck that represents the most positive side of our national character: we have "the spirit to draw on."

The game is the real national anthem of Canada. At any one moment, many thousands of us are all playing hockey, skating our hearts out each day and long into the night from November through April. Hockey is a great unifying symbol of Canada, at the core of the Canadian experience, what Peter Gzowski in *The Game of Our Lives* calls "the common Canadian coin."

The game represents the most important aspects of the national spirit in that it mixes the right amounts of innocence and integrity in a character mould that is elementally Canadian. We take great pains not to admit it — especially to ourselves — but the game of hockey has a powerful hold on the Canadian psyche.

The Sheer Joy of Shinny

... and sometimes on hard-crusted winter snow I've seen the game escape its limits, and leap the width and breadth of things, become a mad chase going nowhere, out past dangerous places ...
— Al Purdy, "The Time of Your Life"

... how much can you teach a ten-year-old? ... There's only so much he's going to take in. Do the basics — that's all they do (in Russia). You see a ten-year-old team in Canada and all you hear is "Shoot! Stay on your wing! Forecheck! Dump it in! Up and out!" The Soviets get all their ten-year-olds on the ice and say "Play shinny ... "
— Wayne Gretzky

Shinny was the first delight of the first people. Among the native Wichita, the first man, whose name was Darkness, was guided to the Light by the flight of a shinny ball.

The game was played on a hard level of beach laid bare by the spring ebb tides. A Clackamas Chinook tale begins: "People lived there .... They played shinny all day long. When it became evening the children were still playing. The villagers told them in vain, 'Quit now. It is night now.' They did not

39

listen. They played only the more: They said to them, 'It might happen that you scare out something there if you don't go inside at dusk.'''

Another myth tells how everyone in the village played together ''at shinny ball, its name is shinny stick. The stick is bent. Once it goes to the goal each period, the wooden shinny ball. On each side are ten men, and so twenty men, young men, played shinny. And that was very dangerous, long ago it was a bad game. If he was hit by a shinny stick, he would split open, his hand would be broken open. He might be struck by the wooden shinny ball in the head or face, he would be split open on his chest. If he got hit he would be bruised. And too some men hit each other, they fought. It was bad to play shinny ball.'' Obviously shinny had a reputation not unlike hockey had in the 1970s. In a later West Coast tale, the face of Wildcat is smashed into its present shape by a shinny stick.

We need no anthropologists to tell us that the shinny stick may have been analogous to the club of the war gods or that it was often seen as the male artifact. Animals often joined the game and played with their tails. You were not allowed to hit your opponent over the head but you were allowed to upset your fellow players by running against them and checking them to the ground.

The shinny ball was not the dirty grey tennis ball we use on the street today. In fact in some native societies the shinny ball of shining wood represented the sun. It was often made of a wood-knot of cedar bark or of buckskin decorated with elaborate bead work. It could not be touched with the hand but could be struck or kicked with the stick or foot. The shinny stick was invariably curved and expanded at the shooting end (one thinks of a lacrosse stick or the machine-made curve of our modern blade) and was sometimes painted or carved. Up until the

1860s the game was played with a ball much like a lacrosse ball.

From this mythic beginning it is easy to see shinny as a symbolic play of life, a realized ancient ritual *and* a carefree improvised game, taking us back to an unknown ancestral past. It was — and is — played in all northern countries, even in Scotland where the word originated from Scottish dialect to depict the whack of the stick against the shin, though our own Iroquois and Algonquin lay equal claim to this hypothesis.

In his book *Hockey Night in Canada*, Foster Hewitt traces shinny's first home back to the Greeks of 500 B.C. Certainly ancient Danes and twelfth-century Anglo-Saxons attached bones to their feet and skated. It is not improbable that they took field hockey sticks out on that same ice. In *Open Net*, George Plimpton pays homage to the patron saint of skaters, Saint Sydarina of Schieden, shown wearing skates in an early fifteenth-century Dutch illustration. The woodcut shows her falling to the ice; the caption tells us she broke a rib. She could have used a hockey stick for support. And early eighteenth-century Dutch have artistic evidence of ''Figures a la mode'' with bone skates and wooden sticks.

It would seem the games of ball hockey, bandy, hurley, and shinty have been around a long time. Private papers, letters, and legends tell us that English troops played the game in Canada as far back as 1783. In his book, Hewitt quotes a nineteenth century historian: ''Most of the soldier boys were quite at home on skates. They could cut the figure eight and other fancy figures, but shinny was their first delight.'' Not long ago Allen Abel reported from Siberia of Russian boys who batted ''an orange ball about the frozen taiga ... using splintered sticks.'' This ''outdoor progenitor of Soviet hockey (is) played by teams of 11 tireless men on enormous expanses of ice.'' The wide-open shinny that results from such free-flowing contests develops the skills of controlling the puck, stickhandling, and pinpoint passing seldom seen in the NHL these days. The huge ice surface also lends itself to the back-tracking, criss-crossing, and weaving that Russian national teams excel in. Abel reports that the Soviet Union has even held international bandy tournaments, hosting teams from the U.S. and Europe, but Canada, where shinny and floor-hockey are played by millions, young and old, has never entered a team.

Everyone who ever played hockey has memories of shinny called pond hockey, street hockey, or boot hockey, depending on what part of the country you grew up in. A friend of mine remembers how he used to go to senior hockey games and ''hang around the players' benches to collect the broken hockey sticks for road hockey or 'horse apples' as it used to be called. With some shellac and tape we'd fix those sticks up for shinny. In those days a stick cost $1.75, which was a day's pay. It was very expensive. A CCM bicycle was $48.00 (we're speaking of the mid-30s) and the minimum wage prior to the war was that much per month. So you took good care of those discarded hockey sticks.''

They always came at midnight. It was as mysterious to us as Santa Claus. As kids, and later as teenagers, we'd wait with rising anticipation and increasing tension as November drew near. Each day it grew colder. We'd walk our regular route to school, then suddenly detour the necessary few blocks to see if the municipal employees we called ''park workies'' had put up the boards and strung the lights. Each night, on the pretense of phoning one another to discuss a problem in our algebra home-work, a two-word message, indecipherable to parents, was whispered as a sign-off: ''Not yet.''

The freezing days of early winter were welcomed with a conviction that could only come from winter people. How many mornings did our skates and sticks become an army of makeshift shovels scraping and flaying the protective snow to reveal the mirror-like surface beneath? At one time Montreal had over 250 outdoor hockey rinks scattered throughout the city. Most of these were in parks; a few were parking lots that would remain icy all winter.

One grew into shinny; it was a coming out of the house and a coming of age on the street. Now one had to perform. The fact that we were out on the street and not yet on the ice didn't matter. We were on stage, performing the epistle according to Foster Hewitt. Shinny is sheer fun, the comedy of ice hockey. The attraction of shinny is the comradeship. Yet even in shinny there is the sense of preparing for battle, putting on the equipment and reaching for the tools of the gladiator. Perhaps the comradeship is there because of the sense of preparing for battle. Other sports, such as football, operate out of lockers; in those early days hockey meant open space.

Shinny begins in the street. David Moore, a friend of mine from Montreal, recalls: ''For us it was Wicksteed Avenue. It was a residential street, close enough to the group of us that usually got together. The major hockey rink was just down the street; while our game of shinny was in progress, we could see the lights of the hockey rink and that added something to the magic of the night.

''I played with Trevor Sevigny—who we called Sevenaxe—and David Chown, who had one brother who hit the big time with the football Alouettes. Sometimes the younger Chowns would come along but usually it was Sevigny, Chown, Leslie Arter, John Stafford, who came all the way from Balfour

Avenue several blocks away, and Doug Stafford, Doug Lawson, and me. Within that group there were sub-groups who would often band together, or sometimes, as in the game of Risk, make alliances to rule the world and then, in midstream, stab their neighbour in the back. And so it is with shinny. That's why it was so important to have one's friendships solid before the game began. In the midst of a play — in mid-stride — you could unexpectedly lose a trusted ally.

"If you had a good friend, as I had in Doug Lawson — the two of us were loners — well, we had a friendship that survived shinny and survived many changes of life. Each time we showed up at one of these shinny games I knew that he would cover my back and that I would cover his. When he got the ball he'd look around for me to whack it to. We always played with a tennis ball, of course, a frozen, ugly, unforgiving, little tennis ball. If it hit you in a place where you were unprotected it could really sting.

"But what I remember lovingly about the game of shinny was the galloping and the sound of the boots on the snow. I never could afford a pair of aviator boots that most kids wore. All my friends had them but Doug Lawson and I came from more straight-laced homes where aviator boots were not seen to be a necessity of life. We couldn't afford the ones with the flaps that came down that had such authority and looked so casual.

"Lawson was nicknamed Rat, a name which has followed him through life among the people who knew him back then. He would stand close to the goal and deflect others' shots into the net. He got to be quite good at that; it was his speciality. As soon as he saw that the play was coming toward the other goal he would run and stand beside it. The goalie would, of course, venture out to cut down the angle, risking much more than a goalie would in hockey. The game of shinny was all about risk, and taking phenomenal chances. The goalie would venture too far out and Rat would tip it in.

"Rat and I would go to these games with a feeling that we would be co-operating in some way, helping each other through. This was never spoken of, just a sense that was there. He was my friend, therefore he would pass it to me and I would pass it to him. And we would be more aware of one another. In the tumult of a shinny game — especially one in which there wasn't much room to manoeuvre — you had to be especially aware of certain people for there to be any kind of co-operation. There were no uniforms; everyone was dressed roughly the same. It was very confusing. In mid-play you might forget who was on your team. Often, it didn't matter.

"It was really a very egotistical game. There was very little room for skillful team play; there was a lot of digging for the ball. Shinny is a lot like rugger as opposed to football. You dug for the ball and once you got it you had a breakaway. And if someone was in the right position you passed it to them.

"It was so comic because there was so little manoeuverability. Shinny is comedy; flopping down to block a shot, stampeding down the ice, breakaways, lunging after the person with the ball and knocking him down rather than really going for the ball sometimes.

"We considered it a manly game. You had to like physical contact. You couldn't complain if you were knocked off your feet. There were no rules. You could trip a guy; it was considered a little gauche but it was okay at the same time. If you had to you had to.

"As for equipment, well, you were certainly not expected to turn up at a shinny game with a new stick. In fact it was probably better to turn up with the stub of a stick. A new stick spoke of a high seriousness which the game did not have. There was a violation if the game was approached in that manner. It just wasn't shinny. It was the same attitude that was reflected in the boot flaps being left down. You had a studied indifference to form. An indifference to rule, order; chaos itself.

''When I think of shinny I especially remember playing at night. The streetlights were higher than they are now. It was very dark. It was a still night and yet there were some flakes that appeared from somewhere and were illuminated by the light before they fell to the ground. In this serene environment we charged up and down on this short patch of slippery, snowy street, every now and then pausing to allow the occasional car through, as if we were a roadblock. We were surrounded by silence and darkness except for the lights of the houses on both sides of the street and the odd pedestrian. We felt quite alone. And there we were, seven or eight of us.

''Teams were seldom even. This is very Canadian. Trevor Sevigny is on one side and on the other, to make up for him, there were two guys to even things out. There was a balance of ability. We could gauge to a fine point who was able to do what and their relative merits in the game. We often had five against seven and were still equal.

''There was very little you could do about changing your status in terms of how you were valued in the minds of the other players. I remember at times feeling on the verge of shinny greatness, having a good night and popping in many goals, but I knew for a fact that this was not going to continue, that this was just a flash-in-the-pan. And the actions and the approaches of the other players to me, in my moment of success, was 'Oh, you got lucky' or 'Ah, what's the matter with you? How come you're this way tonight?' I felt a controlling mechanism was at work, a kind of balance that controlled the subtle status quo of who was worth what in the game of shinny. In life I've seen that same balance at work in myself and in others.

"There were often people falling over, people hitting the street. We became quite intimate with the street. Sticks were used for balance but they were also used as much to trip and slash. There was a great deal of slashing. We used to flip or flick the ball from person to person, not the sort of play you would make on ice. You could count on there being a rut or a frozen ball of sand or some salt in the way to inhibit a smooth clean pass. You were always hampered by the physical conditions.

"And so the best thing you could do would be to golf or slash-swing at the ball with a great big wind-up. This wonderful wind-up was considered a major part of the sheer joy of shinny. You would wind up and whack the ball back from halfway down the ice, the snowflakes flying. Then there would be a pile-up of bodies as people dove after you to try and deflect your aim. Very seldom did we ever try anything in the way of subtle plays. It was grab the ball and try and get it in any way you can. If you hit it with your hand that was all right, kicking, slashing, digging.

"From the chaos in the corners in shinny you learned how to be aggressive, how to keep digging, how to be constantly alert, how to take advantage of an opportunity. We knew that whatever happened it wouldn't last for more than a second or two before the others were on us. You'd dig out the ball and start up, start running but instead of blades on your feet you had these slippery rubber boots. The comic element was that once you did get control — for that one brief second — of that slippery little ball it would not last for long; all the others would recoup and come after you before you got up a head of steam.

47

"Once you did get up a head of steam you were a force to be reckoned with and your momentum would keep you going.

"If the rink or road area were already occupied by skaters and hockey players, we shinny players would loom up over the horizon of the snowbank like Cossacks prior to attack and plop on the ice. It was the chaotic aspect of the aviator boots. We were like Huns. We would just stand there. It was the force of our presence, plus our numbers. We had won the ice. Usually, after a few minutes, the skaters took off their skates and joined us. Even the best hockey players were always more than willing to play shinny. And some of the great shinny players like John Atkinson never played hockey because they had weak ankles. John's ankles would flop over and get tired and so he could never skate well. The hierarchy of shinny was such that you could play the game well and never play hockey and still be honoured as a hockey player. It was the business about not taking yourself seriously, not taking the game seriously. It really didn't matter and yet we all knew it did. It's like being in school and doing well according to school rules and being accepted by the teachers as opposed to doing well in what's important to your peer group.

"After surviving a shinny match, hockey players felt that anything that happened to them in a hockey game was routine. This gave the hockey player a far better attitude toward body-checking when he played the game on ice. It gave him a healthy disposition toward checking virtually absent in hockey today. He became accustomed to it and in a strange way looked forward to it. Handing out a good check is a wonderful feeling. There's nothing quite so clean and satisfying as knocking someone entirely off their feet with a good check when they least expect it. And it would soon be your turn. But that didn't matter. People are prepared to be just in shinny."

The Sheer Joy of Shinny

John Tonelli, one of the heroes of Team Canada's
1984 victory over the Russians, thinks he developed
his relentless style as a child when his brother...
took him to play winters on community rinks,
summers on the street with a tennis ball.

Trent Frayne, *Globe and Mail*

"When you say shinny do you mean street hockey?"
asks Victoria schoolteacher Winston Jackson. "We played
spring, summer, and fall on roller skates in the street. These
skates had heavy metal wheels, unlike the wooden or high
density rubber ones now. They sounded great. If you were in
goal it was like an express train coming at you.

"We played with hockey sticks, a tennis ball, and orange
juice tins as goals (whereas kids on the Prairies used scrap
wood and grain sacks). In our milder climate here on the West
Coast we were trying to emulate what it was like under "real"
conditions. If we were feeling professional and wanted to play a
wide sweeping game we'd go to a Safeway parking lot with a
big wall behind so one didn't have to be concerned about
having to fetch a missed shot. Safeway stores did their parking
lots very, very smoothly. On the road you took your chances.
Cars didn't matter. But there were some rough surfaces,
especially those with pea-gravel in the tar. This slowed the
game down. The city tarred the street and sprinkled pea-gravel
on and rolled it in with a steamroller. That was "slow ice."
And if we got an outdoor lacrosse court they were really
smooth, smoother than even the Safeway lots.

"One guy had a goalie stick and we took turns in nets. We'd
all borrow the one cup and strap it on to the outside of our jeans.
(You couldn't take off your pants and stick it inside!) It made
us feel big. We had something to protect. It made us like men.

"We all followed the NHL. It was like a play in which we took all the parts. We'd fight over roles: 'This time I get to be Nesterenko,' that sort of thing. In *The Game* Dryden wrote of how as a young boy, he played in the NHL inside his head, the hero of all his own games. We all played that endless fantasy and we all heard Foster Hewitt call our name. We'd play and then we'd listen to the Stanley Cup finals on the radio. Everyone followed either Montreal or Toronto."

Jackson remembers skating outdoors for the first time during a rare "freeze-over" in Victoria: "The first thing we all did was fall flat on our backs; our skates weren't sharp enough for the real thing. If and when a freeze-up occurred all the ponds out in the countryside turned to ice. The word went out that Panama Flats was frozen over and suddenly there were a hundred kids playing hockey. I still don't know how we got out to those places. The hockey players were at one end of the flats, skaters at the other, a bonfire in the middle. But hockey was something done in strange places; back East and on the Prairies. That's where 'they did it.' We just tried as best we could to imitate it. Yet there was a hockey history on the west coast. I remember the Penticton Vees and the Trail Smoke Eaters, the Vees and the Smokies. The big event every year was when the Canadian team was chosen to play the Russians. For us kids hearing a series against the Russians was like listening to the moon landing.

"By the time we were between 12 and 14 years old and in junior high the early morning trips to the arena for ice-time before classes was beginning to kill many of us. But we loved doing it because it was seen as such a neat thing to do; to arrive at school, sweaty and red-faced, and to be seen putting your skates and stick in your locker. Being seen was everything.

"But the biggest thrill for us street hockey kids was to go

down to the ocean off Dallas Road when the Harrison Yacht Pond froze over. It had finally arrived, real hockey, pucks. And we'd return at night. Shooting a real puck in the moonlight.''

Shinny is now played year-round, the result of our increasing drift away from a sense of the natural seasons and rhythms of life. The game of winter still contains some icy features though, in spite of its recent adaptation. Summer tennis balls are kept in mother's freezer to give the ball a better spin and make it dip. And summer shinny still has the sting of the winter game. It hurts. Some feel that summer shinny is even rougher than hockey or winter shinny because it is played with no equipment at all on a concrete or paved surface. In this respect summer shinny is closer to lacrosse than hockey. My nephews and their friends have the best of all possible worlds. They set up deliberately in the parking lot between the municipal swimming pool and the hockey arena. They can freeze the tennis balls in the ice-pile left by the Zamboni and play the game, with their girlfriends in the pool as spectators.

Wherever and whenever shinny is played there are never any referees; players are always on their own honour and various unwritten codes of conduct prevail. It is left to the players themselves to work out things between them. Perhaps this is why hockey players of an earlier era had a greater sense of sportsmanship than young players today.

Now there are organized winter shinny leagues in many parts of the country, the result of our compulsion to organize everything in our lives. Organized shinny is a contradiction in terms; it takes away the very spontaneity that is the chief attraction of the game. In Winnipeg bars I heard stories of the times when Bobby Hull, known as ''The Golden Jet,'' would drive by an open-air rink after a WHA game, and park his car so that the headlights shone on the icy surface. After a few minutes of practising his famous slapshot, kids from the neighbourhood would materialize out of the darkness, sticks in hand, and Hull would play shinny with them.

Kids now play with a plastic orange puck on outdoor ice, if the latter can be found. There is no more impulsive phone call from the first kid who is struck by the sudden urge to be out on the ice with his friends battling the cold and a frozen tennis ball for the sheer joy of shinny. And there is no chain reaction of phone calls that, at an appointed time, suddenly brings 20 kids from all directions leaping from snowbanks onto the ice to take it over for two hours on a bright, icy Sunday afternoon to play a game without rules, referees, and time limit, in fact few limitations of any kind.

In this country where hockey is both hell and a holy thing, shinny is different. Shinny is where you can loiter on defence, or giggle at the outrageous moves of your opponents. You are taking the game too seriously if you keep score. A team is always one-up or four-up — the margin of three or four grunted out in a single syllable immediately after a goal is scored as the triumphant goal-scorer and his teammates turn up ice. If some god was keeping score he would need a pair of calculators. The nonchalance of shinny is one of its greatest attractions. You appear to be nonchalant but you're trying like hell. You always took it seriously, but were instantly able to stand back and look at yourself in a self-deprecating manner. The happy-go-lucky approach was never far beneath the surface. The paradox is obvious but true: it doesn't matter but it matters a great deal.

Playing only shinny, the game was particularly important to John Atkinson. It was his one chance to excel. One day he appeared at the rink a few minutes after we'd begun playing.

He sat on the edge of the boards, feigning nonchalance until a break in the action made it possible for him to join us. I was in nets. He came back to me, a wry smile on his face I couldn't figure out, then went to centre to play for the opposing team. He got the draw. Suddenly I heard a strange sound. It was as if the ice was being cut open. I saw Atkinson weaving in on me, going around our centreman and the defence like they weren't there. He was putting moves on them I'd never seen before, moves that were impossible to make wearing rubber boots. As he bore in on me the sound of crunched ice grew louder. Atkinson put four or five moves on me before depositing his shot in the back of the net. There was a stunned silence. All of us stared at the ice. It had been cut up into squares as if some prehistoric animal dying of thirst had attempted to eat the ice. Atkinson's trail from centre could easily be traced. Several of us jumped him, holding him down while we examined his up-turned boots. Four metal clips were attached to each sole. There may well have been no rules in shinny, but this was going too far. I can't remember when we laughed so long and so hard. John joined in the laughter, then changed into his shoes to finish the game. It was a great moment in shinny history.

Each moment is played for the particular moment; each moment of improvised action that results in a goal or a great save is held, savoured, suspended in time, and celebrated with a warming rush of adrenalin until the next great play is made. The only boundaries are personal to each player: degree of interest, ability, intensity, and physical stamina. The joy we feel when we make a great move comes from the unconscious sense that we are at the fullest extension of our natural abilities, our human powers. We are as at one with nature and each other as we will ever be, self-worth and personal dignity in the unconscious core of each one of us playing the game, for we know our chance to excel will come and we will take our place in the confraternity created by this universal game. In the meantime, between these high moments, the combined arts of stickhandling, controlling the ball, receiving a pass, avoiding a bodycheck, dishing one out, manoeuvering to get into the clear, learning how to rag the puck, and developing one's defensive skills — as well as the offensive skills of slashing, hooking, holding, and tripping — these are all practised, polished and occasionally perfected in a game that dishes out fun and friendship in equal doses.

Life On Ice?

Hockey is so much fun... Maybe it's just as well that I live in a penthouse. If I lived at street-level in Edmonton, the winter would come and I'd look out the window at the kids playing road hockey, and before you know it I'd be out there with them.

— **Wayne Gretzky**

When the great feene is frozen young men play upon the yee. Some tye bones to their feets and shoving themselves by a little picked staffe, doe slide as swiftly as an arrow out of a cross bow. Sometimes two runne together with poles and one doth fall, not without hurt. Youth desirous of glorie, in this sport exerciseth itself against the time of warre.

— **Secretary to Thomas à Becket**

Hockey at its best is high drama, as exciting and unpredictable as life. Not the hockey we see on television, not even what we see from an expensive rink-side seat. But anyone who watches from the catwalk or gondola, or up in the nose-bleeds, sees 12 players on a 200-foot stage. From such a vantage point, way above the circling players, looking directly down on them, you can see the centre a second or two before he picks up the

puck on a power play, and spot the free winger who will eventually get the puck wheeling over the blueline uncovered, as both defencemen rush to check the centre and the other wing.From this height the swirling players form a ballet on ice.

When two hockey teams tangle, they represent two different communities, two cities or — the way we like it best — two countries. Hockey is founded upon a dramatic, a human relation. The entire spectacle may be seen as a series of individual, isolated moves, each self-contained but all interrelated, one frame after another adding up to the whole. Significant form. Style. A sense of beauty. The perfection of motion. The flow. The eye for the line. The common obsession with the game we all share.

As fans we identify with a Beliveau, Orr, Lafleur, or Gretzky as with a god, however guilty we feel for harbouring such mythic illusions. Superstars serve a variety of purposes for the average hockey fan, in the largest sense offering an escape from the reality of life and death, but, chiefly, representing an ideal, a fantasy of what the fan, ''desirous of glorie,'' might have become.

In a year-ending poll conducted by *Maclean's* magazine, respondents were invited to imagine ''they could achieve world-class success in one of five fields — acting, business, politics, sports, or writing.'' Business was, of course, the first choice of Canadians at 35 per cent, followed, amazingly enough, by writing (26 per cent), and sports at 21. Of the Canadian men who chose sports, hockey was their overwhelming first choice.

Even movie stars want to be hockey heroes. Burnaby's own Michael J Fox, star of movies and TV, recently registered a hat-trick in a charity game against the Minnesota North Stars. Fox said his ambition was to play on the same line as

Stan Mikita. "It's a Canadian boy's dream."

It is clear that the Howes and Richards give us not merely wish-fulfillment but possibility, however remote: the possibility of full human experience. For the individual player, such as Bobby Hull, the reality may indeed be something quite different. The fan knows this, but it is what Hull represents that matters, his reflection on the ice. Even the journeyman player offers hope for heroism, just by being there. If a fan can't identify with the god-like talents of the superstar in this age of anti-heroes, he has no difficulty feeling at one with a journeyman pork chopper. In addition, the fan sees that such a player remains unchanged by his brush with greatness. He's still one of us.

It is a simple leap from personal to national identification ("fan" is short for "fanatic"). A university student explained to me that tragedy struck the nation after game two of Rendez-Vous '87. His country was disgraced, we'd lost in combat. He wrote that "the weapons were sticks, the ammunition a puck, the target a net and 22 men in red inflicted the damage." He went on: "I've lost hundreds of times in the last 24 hours since the end of the game. This is what it's like when somebody dies."

Although later he felt his position had been extreme, he confessed to always feeling that, whenever Canada played the Soviet Union, the outcome mattered to the entire country. "For once we were united in one cause," he wrote, and then thought of "how ludicrous it was that a simple game can have that effect when few other issues can overcome our geographical, language, and cultural barriers."

But hockey is our way of life, a common denominator that Canadians rally around, though some do not understand why we spend so much time, effort, and money on the game. Solon, a symbol of the wise man and successful politician in Ancient Greece had the answer centuries ago when he said, "You would have to be there":

> By seeing what was going on you would be able to appreciate that we are quite justified in expending so much ardour on these spectacles. I cannot find words to give you an idea of the pleasure that you would have if you were seated in the middle of the anxious spectators, watching the courage of the athletes, the beauty of their bodies, their splendid poses, their extraordinary suppleness, their tireless energy, their audacity, their sense of competition, their unconquerable courage, their unceasing efforts to win a victory. I am sure that you would not cease to overwhelm them with praise, to shout again and again, to applaud.

We in Canada suffer from an intellectual snobbery where hockey is concerned. In Canada, the arts and intellectual life are as far removed from sport as one can imagine. For the Greeks, the games of sport were not separated from cultural and intellectual events. In those ancient times, successful athletes brought prestige and honour to the town or city they represented. At the time of the Greek city-states, a portion of the city wall was broken down after an athletic victory, for no city required a wall around itself when it had such athletes to defend it.

Once asked by a reporter what attracted him to the game, Eric Nesterenko exclaimed: "To really move was my delight."

Hockey is the very apogee of physical action, the only sport to allow substitutions on the fly. On ice, skating all out, head up, full thighs lifting the legs up, up 'til we can hardly feel them, we almost take flight. Indeed, there were times when Guy Lafleur looked more like Mercury than mere mortal.

Playing the game all-out offers many rewards, but the feeling of release, of individual freedom, must be at or near the top of everyone's list. Nesterenko referred to this as "the sweetness in being able to move and control your body," but there is more to it than that. The game has an elemental purity; the individual confronting the natural hardness of ice and cold and emerging victorious. Each time we score, whether in a game or playing alone, taking shots on an empty net, a personal, undeclared, momentary celebration takes place, a celebration of our own skill that results in a feeling of exhilaration, excitement, a coursing of the blood. I can still hear the puck snapping into the chickenwire. Even in practise, alone on the ice, there is a thrill in taking 20 shots and having the 18th be pure perfection, the stick brought back just so...the whoosh of the puck. At these times we feel a surge of energy; we feel life itself flowing through our bodies. We have found our better selves.

Is it for the love of hockey or is it the hope of being adolescent forever that keeps us playing long past our prime, our quest for eternal youth, the shared interest or common bonding its greatest attraction? It is out on the ice that the child in us plays. Money problems, family quarrels, business concerns — all left behind. Here, things are closer, the world is clear, white, transparent, understandable.

How one plays the game determines how one plays in life. These values are transferable. The game is an education. French writer Albert Camus put it best: "Sport was the main occupation of all of us, and continued to be for a long time. That is where I had my only lesson in ethics."

If we're not playing, watching such a spectacle can be almost as exciting, especially for a youngster. The sense of anticipation knows no boundaries. Some kids will do anything to see a game. Donald Braden recalls what lengths he and his friends went to in Camrose, Alberta, before the invention of the Zamboni: "To watch the senior team in town we would scrape the ice so we could get into the game; we were like a volunteer fire department. We'd put five scrapers on the ice at a time and a couple of guys to haul the snow away at the end. We'd use five guys in a row pushing into the middle in smaller and smaller circles."

As we get older, we want to recapture our skills in our imagination for a fleeting moment, to recapture the memories of a simpler life on the ice.

> In winter, when I owned my first pair of skates
> and kept falling down repeatedly, we chased an old
> tin can or lump of coal on the frozen river, batting
> at it with a broken board, or an old hockey stick if
> we were lucky. When the river was clear of snow,
> the game sometimes took on wider dimensions.
> A fast skater might stickhandle clear of the small
> boy ruck, making for the bridge and under it to the
> bay; a coloured screaming rabble of children pur-
> suing him .... And far out there on the black ice,
> alone, in really cold weather the ice would rumble
> and crack with the sound of eternity. I'd stand
> there shivering, knowing there were monsters
> waiting, looking at me under the ice. See their
> shadows wavering back and forth behind the ice
> barrier, hungry. And notice also another boy
> watching me, red-nosed from the cold, lifting his

hand when I lift my hand, uncannily like myself but
not myself, reflected on the ice.

— Al Purdy,
Morning and It's Summer

All of this is well and good, but there is another side to the
game. A player matures and is eligible to be drafted by the
NHL about the time he graduates from high school. Choosing
a career in the NHL, he effectively puts his education behind
him. The often-referred-to Dr Randy Gregg, formerly of the
Oilers, is a notable exception; only eight per cent of NHL
players have college diplomas.

As attractive as the fusion of personal skills with the needs
of the team may be, there are negative consequences. The
modern hockey player-athlete leads a very protected life. Freed
by his huge salary from having to meet everyday responsibilities,
he lives a cocoon-like existence. As a result, a player quickly
develops a distorted outlook on life, a distortion that leaves him
unprepared for a world away from ice. The warning in EM
Forster's *A Passage to India* is an ominous one: ''The fire of
fellowship in their eyes ... cooled with their bodies, for athletics
can only raise a temporary glow.''

As well, the constant pressure of having to achieve, both
as an individual and as a team, can be overwhelming in a sport
where one has the opportunity to fail all the time. The puck
may be constantly out of reach. Physical fear is rarely thought
of but psychological fear, the fear of personal and team failure,
is constant.

The game proved to be a destructive influence on Claudia
Thompson's son. The dream was okay, she told me when I
interviewed her, but it wasn't her son's dream, it was always

65

someone else's — his father's, his friends', his coach's. Unreal expectations were created.

A father may inflict an opposite and equally difficult pressure upon the son: the game will teach him to become a man. The father, who may never have been that good when he played, sees the possibility of his aspirations being realized through his son. The son tries to perform for the father; this in direct conflict with what the mother wants. She constantly stresses good play and sportsmanship — and for him always to be careful — while the father sits in the stands and shouts, ''Move the puck ... Shoot ... Be aggressive ... Take control ... Hit the guy.''

For some boys, nature makes the decision. That's what happened to Claudia Thompson's son: he simply grew too tall and angular, too uncoordinated. Other boys are drawn away from hockey as they grow older: they turn to other sports, get a part-time job or a full-time girlfriend, or simply tire of the game.

Some realize their dream and make the NHL. And some of these see the dream turn to a nightmare when they leave the game. When a player's talents go, he goes; he feels a failure. What's worse, his situation is there for all to see. For many NHLers, there is nothing beyond playing. Fred Shero, former coach of the Flyers, put it best when he said: ''Life is just a place where we spend time between games.''

Winning is hard work. The true champion goes beyond himself. He accepts no limits, either to what he can do or what he will endure. It is always easier to lose. Especially when it makes little or no difference to your inflated paycheque.

If you get used to losing, you lose more than a hockey game or two. You can lose your professional career. The erosion of confidence, the loss of personal drive carry over into life. Some players try so hard not to lose they have no chance of winning. Others simply self-destruct in tense circumstances. They have an unconscious will to lose. Many highly competitive sports, such as squash, pit the player against himself as much as his opponent. Dr Edmund Bergler of New York coined the phrase ''psychic masochism'' for this self-defeating tendency. In such cases victory means victory over oneself.

Often, in international competition — with the notable exceptions of our outstanding Canada Cup stars — our patched-together teams perform a disappearing act and willingly succumb to the repeated rushes of the Soviets and Czechs. Like all adolescents, we play well when in command, but fall apart when we fall behind. According to political scientist Arthur Kroker, it is the Canadian Protestant mind doing what it likes to do best — ''losing in a world in which the deck is stacked against them.'' Peter Newman has noted our ''genetic affinity for discomfort and self-denial.'' And it was Earle Birney who once described our country on ice as ''a high school land, frozen in its adolescence.''

Some players — indeed, some teams — unconsciously relish the role of martyrdom. Witness the Detroit Red Wings in the '87 Stanley Cup quarter-final against Edmonton. We have a particular empathy for playing the martyr and embracing the underdog. Red Wing coach Jacques Demers lavished such fulsome praise on the Oilers one would have thought the latter would be embarrassed to even show up for the series. While the tactic is obviously to lull the other team into a state of lethargy, at a deeper level Demers was preparing the boys to lose. However, if the Red Wings had won under such circumstances, well, you're more than a giant-killer, you're a giant. It's difficult to lose psychologically playing under these conditions. And that's the idea. If you do, you go down in a blaze of glory, the honour of your team intact.

When you play on a losing team for a long time you simply give up after a while. You continue to play hard but you play without passion or fire. You give up mentally — you simply don't expect to win and you don't. In Olympic circles, Canada is sometimes known as "the home of the bronze medal." Attitude is the key element and, on a losing team, it's the most difficult thing to sustain. You play a different game on a winning team than with a loser. I think particularly of Cam Neeley, an unfulfilled promise with the Canucks, who blossomed into a prolific goal scorer and fine all-around player when he joined the Bruins. Some respond to the exhilaration of the challenge. Some don't and grow complacent. "There is something remarkably strong about a team that wins; and something remarkably weak about the same team when it doesn't," Ken Dryden wrote in *The Game*.

"I feel we worked as hard as we could. We're pretty proud to come out 1 - 1," said Wayne Gretzky after the two-game Rendez-Vous '87 showdown. This should never have been an acceptable result. We tied 1 - 1 in games. How could anyone possibly be "proud" of this result? Only because we've lost in international competition so often that we now feel proud of a tie.

In the world hockey championships held in Vienna, the Canadian team won 3 out of the 10 games they played, and lost any chance they had of a medal when Sweden, who won the gold for the first time in 25 years, blew our players out of the rink, 9 - 0. After the final game, defenceman Craig Hartsburg, who personally played extremely well, commented: "We played our hearts out in this tournament. The 23 guys we have here should hold their heads high. We played as hard as we could. We've got nothing to be ashamed of. I hope nobody feels we've disgraced anybody.'' He was wrong. But how can we blame him? What country in their right mind would send players from teams in the bottom half of their league to represent them?

Some say that hockey is like life: we go there to see life played out in some symbolic sense — the players as types or characters on a stage, by turns violent, entertaining, heroic, and comic. This is true. Others say that hockey is an escape. We go there to escape the humdrum, to worship our heroes and see them play out our fantasies. We seek the illusion. This is also true. It's as if we're playing a trick on ourselves. We go to the thing as if it is an escape, and find when we're there that it's very much like life.We're simply sneaking in the back door of our own psyche, buying a ticket to the other side of our national character — the world of risk, danger, and abandon.

Montserrat Gonzalez of Burgos, Spain, has lived in Canada for the past 20 years. She went to her first and last hockey game in 1979 at the Northlands Coliseum in Edmonton. What she saw chills her still. Perhaps it takes a Spaniard to see most deeply into the Canadian character.

''The arena was full of people. Once the game started the atmosphere changed. What I saw was not so much a game with two teams playing and spectators watching as a ritual where all was one; there was no difference between the players and the spectators. People were not observing some activity going on that happened to be a sport; these were people going through an experience, a shared experience. They were all united. The feeling was so strong. I looked around and saw people from different walks of life, some wearing a suit and tie, some in jeans, different natures, both sexes, but they all were behaving in the same way. They were behaving the same way because they were feeling the same way.

"What I saw was so violent that I wanted to hide. I actually thought of going under the seats. Then I realized, what am I thinking of? I'm supposed to be watching something that is the national sport. I shouldn't be afraid. My logic was saying you don't have to be but my feelings were saying, hide, this is dangerous. I was surprised to feel this way. I kept looking around for a sign to reassure me that everything was okay, that this was just a sport.

"But I couldn't find any. The audience was totally oblivious of what was happening. They weren't aware of what was going on, neither the players nor the spectators. It was an unconscious, spontaneous sharing. Nothing was checked or withheld. It just came out. They couldn't help it, you could see it. It had to be. That was the way it was.

"It was like an agreed-upon ritual. It was like birth has to be, and death. It was a ritual that was taking place because of a need in the society, the culture of this country.

"In some ways it was like the Spanish ritual of bull-fighting. The same in that it is a ritual and it is necessary for the survival of the culture. However, the nature of the ritual is different here. In Spain, the bullfight is a ritual of life and death, the celebration of life. In that Edmonton rink that night I was experiencing the ritual of violence, that part of human beings that is violent and manifests itself in war or fighting; in this case it was presented in ritual form, as a hockey game. I had the feeling that the participants did not understand the essence of this ritual but simply that it had to be in order for them to exist as a people, as a country.

"It's not something one can pick up on television; like any ritual you have to be there, you have to experience it live. The hockey rink seemed to be the only place where these people could demonstrate who and what they were. A place where license was allowed. And they knew it was allowed, both on and off the ice. They knew that to feel like this in the arena was okay, was permitted.

"Most people were not aware of the sense of violence because there is little or no blood. It's not like boxing. I was not afraid of the players with their sticks. I was afraid of the people around me, these businessmen, these professionals. I was feeling a violence in the air.

"It surprised me because Canada is so desperate for an image of pacificism and moderation. Canadians try to live up to this but fail because it is false and this false image they project prevents Canadians from finding the real definition of themselves. There was certainly no moderation at the game I saw. Everyone let go. They couldn't help it. It had to be. Hockey seemed to demand it. The power of the game is that it allows us to show — and experience — the other side of our national character without being aware of it.

"In fact, whenever I've tried to talk about this with friends they say no, that's not so, hockey is just a game to us. Well, it may be for other people in other countries but for Canadians it is not simply a sport. And though I've chosen to make your country my home, I've never been to a hockey game again."

Paradoxes and contradictions abound and keep us and the game alive. The game is both spontaneous *and* ordered, both an individual effort *and* good team play at the same time.

To paraphrase poet Al Purdy, hockey is rather like jazz in its improvisation, its imaginative quality; you never know what's coming next. And yet there *are* plays, "what if" situations are endlessly discussed, skills are constantly honed, strategy is planned, then adjusted to fit the particular situation, much like the interplay of life. According to psychologist Marie-Louise von Franz " ... most games are in a way images of life; you can use your reason but you are up against chance.''

When we perform to the highest level of our physical limits and our abilities — then extend ourselves beyond — we feel in harmony, not only with ourselves and the game, but with life itself. Such divine epiphanies, when the synthesis of our skills and the natural momentum of the game become one in a slow unfolding tableau, are almost beyond words. In the '87 Stanley Cup quarter-final playoffs, Detroit Red Wings' goalie Glen Hanlon experienced several such moments. A shy and modest man, he described how it felt at the time: ''When you're in a groove ... things slow down a bit for you. You can almost see the play before it happens.''

At such moments, time not merely slows down but sometimes stops. The next moment, the next game, has no meaning. NOW is everything. You skate on to another level. A split-second after a great save or an outstanding goal everything slows down or is stopped, the moment fixed forever in time (as well as on instant replay). A sense of wholeness and well-being exudes from every pore. There is no greater high.

Rite of Passage

You could race over miles and miles of ice with twenty-foot strides on seven-league skates: you were the next thing to immortal and only ten years old.

— Al Purdy

All sports have a rite of passage; hockey is no exception. Things can happen on the ice that rank as the most significant events in a young man's life before he reaches the age of first love.

Such an initiation occurs around the time of puberty. By then many of us have spent thousands of hours playing shinny in the street, on the neighbourhood rink, or donning the blades for pick-up games where we could improve our skills. It was during one of these games that I found myself on the opposite team from my older brother. We arrived at the rink together, and common sense and hard numbers dictated that each of us went to a different team.

It was during that same game on a Sunday afternoon when the snow was too bright to look at that Dave Ratchford and his father appeared. Were they really there, or am I simply fusing

73

these two incidents for convenience? I don't know if my mind has joined these rites of passage, or whether they really did occur at the same time, but I hold them together now, in my imagination.

Dave Ratchford — "Scratch," as we called him, because he was constantly scratching himself — was an excellent hockey player, a strong fierce-checking defenceman who used his butt as a block or bumper to stop the swiftest skater cold in his tracks. I watched him play on many occasions and knew that he was both tough and fair, what all good hockey players are to fourteen-year-olds, and, perhaps, what they were before the age of windmill hockey sticks and cheap shots. No one had ever seen Scratch's father on skates.

Mr Ratchford was a slight, frail-looking man of average height built like a goalpost. Most of us had all of our equipment on but Mr Ratchford came on ice with a pair of battered CCM skates and dress pants — well-pressed grey flannels that barely covered his lace tops. He sported a small brown windbreaker and the kind of English cap that my grandfather wore at soccer matches in the old country. We were too polite to laugh but it was hard not to grin from behind our gauntlets as we stood at either end of the ice waiting for the game to begin. Someone tossed a puck into our corner and we were off!

There were 15 guys a side, maybe 20 or even more on each team; the ice was swarming with players, all skating after one tiny puck and hacking away at it whenever we got the opportunity.

Scratch and I were on the same team. We saw a lot of each other; he wheeling back toward me after I'd missed yet another check and was busy fishing the puck out of our net. The only time we saw Ratchford Senior was when he slowed down after scoring and glided smoothly by us, expressionless, up the ice.

My brother was an excellent skater and playmaker and there were many fine hockey players in our part of town but I'd never seen anyone skate as fast or handle the puck as well as Mr Ratchford. His acceleration was amazing. When he was moving at top speed — he seemed to know no other — it was as if his skates never touched the ice. He went by in a blur.

He had all the moves. No matter how you came at him he had the uncanny knack of forcing you to make the first move. He simply waited forever, dangling the puck on his stick, sucked you in, then moved around you, leaving you whacking away at the air of his wake. I don't remember how many goals he scored that day before, mercifully, it began to grow dark and we all wound our way home for supper, but it must have been several dozen. Our goalie finally gave up going for the moves that Mr Ratchford put on him and simply stood there, hoping the puck would hit him by mistake. But it never did. And Mr Ratchford never got tired of skating and scoring.

The only thing that was on our side was the law of averages and, late in the afternoon, both Scratch and I experienced our rite of passage in the dying moments of the day.

We'd been spectators for so long that some things were beginning to add up. Also, we were trying so many things that something had to work. Mr Ratchford came at us for the umpteenth time that afternoon, fed at centre by a pinpoint pass from my brother, the kind of pass that appears impossible to reach and yet — taking into account the potential speed of the recipient — hits him in full stride, extended wholly.

The elder Ratchford flew toward his son and I and a half dozen others gathered at the blueline. We approached him as if we were curlers frantically sweeping the ice in front of a potential game-winning shot. We looked like a small army of irritated ants. Mr Ratchford veered close to the right boards

and was about to zip around me when I noticed Scratch coming at his father from the other side of the unruly mass we made — sight unseen and set low to the ice. Scratch turned his butt into his father's speed and lifted the elder Ratchford, sending him spilling high and headfirst into the huge snowbank by the blueline boards. I couldn't help noticing that, though he had not seen the check coming, Mr Ratchford had become one with the force of the blow at the initial moment of impact. He seemed to glide into the snowbank, a soft smile covering his face.

We all stood about, our mouths hanging open breathing smoke. I grabbed the puck and chopped up the near-empty ice on my ankles. It was all open ice to the net until I saw my brother weaving a familiar pattern from the other side of the rink, backskating in that wonderfully fluid style of his, skate over skate, his legs rolling over and over until he'd picked up speed to such an extent he'd gotten between me and the net. He looked like he was sitting there, body open and poised stick forward in a wide arc waiting.

I could no longer see the goaltender, my brother took up so much space. I thought of all he'd taught me and what he might forget. I thought of letting the puck drop off my stick as if by accident, luring him in, then cradling it like a lacrosse ball back and forth between my skates 'til I swept it back up to my stick.

I don't know what I did but it worked. He played the puck and I went harmlessly around him only to see the thing come through his legs and settle on my stick. Having played nets on many occasions, scoring was a mere formality.

To claim both Scratch and I ''did it again'' in the last rush of twilight is to ice the cake and eat it too. But we did. I don't know what went on around the Ratchford dinner table that evening but I suspect something was changed. I do know that as my brother and I trudged home for supper over the town bridge that spanned the railway tracks something had changed. Carrying my kit bag in one hand and my skates strung on my stick in the other my voice was a good octave lower. My body felt transformed, my blood altered. I received a new, quiet respect from my brother. It was in the air, not asked for, simply understood, and given. From such small beginnings other things grow. I was a part of a larger world. The journey had begun. I felt I could go forward. I had come of age on the ice.

Going Back
to the Big Leagues

Wrapped up under the covers. Half fetus, half cocoon. I want to stay here all morning, not moving except to turn over like toast, balancing both sides.

But the bus leaves in one hour and I've got to get to the bus. I leave the bed the way I used to leave the ice; one quick hop and I'm off, the cold morning chill driving me awake.

Why am I doing this I ask myself as I hastily dress. A 45-year-old man boarding with a busload of kids and adolescents heading from Victoria across the Strait of Juan de Fuca on a ferry to see a National Hockey League game. Ridiculous. Why do we do the things we do? Yet it's when one stops to think about what one does naturally that the trouble sets in. It's why hockey players get paid not to think.

The bus is full of close-cropped pimply-faced kids. They seem to come from another era. These are not the kids one sees hanging around corner stores after dark. In fact I haven't seen the likes of these kids for a long time. The talk is of trading hockey cards; of how many autographs can be collected

if we arrive early enough; and of what would happen if there was a bench-clearing brawl and we missed the last ferry back to the island. Gretzky's moves are frequently referred to but not spoken of — language seems to break down, hands holding an imaginary stick are brought into play, a swish swishing sound is made, a ''t'' replacing the ''sw'' sound to simulate the swiftness of Gretzky's puckhandling.

A few fathers are aboard, two or three girls. The former's conversations turn on the talents of Eddie Shore, the latter group on whether Tony Tanti or Patrick Sundstrom is the most handsome Canuck.

Several shopping bags are brought on; soon the whole bus smells like an ad for Molson's Canadian. Two or three cliques form at the back of the bus, each one around a shopping bag. It's half an hour from the city to the ferry terminal and the salty taste of the sea.

I try to get psyched up for this. Vancouver versus Boston, the new era of the general manager behind the bench, Gerry Cheevers replaced by his old friend and GM, Harry Sinden. Two roles couldn't be further apart in hockey or in life than the coach and general manager. The responsibilities are entirely different, yet the NHL has several GMs hard at work attempting to direct players on the ice rather than getting the best players available for the coach. The Canucks' Harry Neale will match wits with Sinden this particular night but neither of them will be where a good GM should be — up in the stands assessing the players or off in some other city or freezing prairie town checking out the best young talent to be had in future drafts.

The ferry ride is smooth, the sun warming, the line of the light making a silver necklace on the water. The bus cliques finally break up; some fans go to the cafeteria, some the newsstand, others wander in the sun on the upper deck. The newsstand opens and there's an edition of *Sports Illustrated* featuring Wayne Gretzky on the cover that makes its way round the ship as fast as Gretzky goes end-to-end. Everyone from the bus converges on the newsstand and the magazine is sold out in a few minutes. Each person buys a copy, even if they are traveling with a friend or two. Clearly, what you know you must know first-hand and make it your own. As well, these copies are bought not simply to be read but to be kept. The kids are collectors — historians of the game they love. Each copy is carefully read, carefully coveted, held, and packed away in the kit bags that seldom leave the hand.

"The Great One Gets Greater" has a picture of The Great One with his girlfriend, Vickie Moss, that sends shivers of jealousy through the teenaged girls making the trip. The boys are excited by the revelation that sportswriter Jack Falla actually skated with Gretzky and coach Sather (another behind-the-bench GM) during a recent Oiler workout in Edmonton. Falla, who still plays pick-up hockey on a regular basis, calls it a privilege and a revelation to skate with The Big G during a morning's workout. The kids read aloud Falla's description of the almost incomprehensible speed of the skaters and how — unlike other Edmonton players — "Gretzky seems to be moving lightly, his skates barely cutting the ice with a snick...snick...snick" sound as compared with the more normal scrunch. These fans read aloud The Great One's assessment of his own unique talent: "What I do is instinctive. I feel my way down the ice. I see where I want to go and I go there. How could I coach that?"

"He doesn't want to be a coach or a GM," shouts one kid as we pile back onto the bus, "he wants to be an owner!"

"Wow, an owner," a friend says. "Imagine owning your

own hockey team. I'd never thought of that!''

I take a last glance at the article, and though I'm glad it's there, that *Sports Illustrated* ran the thing and put The Great One on the cover, I can't help thinking it's an American magazine and that Gretzky gets a scant four pages and five photos (including the close-up cover shot), while a story on playing basketball in Indiana has 30 photographs spread over 22 pages and is really the feature article in the issue. No matter how many teams they have in the National Hockey League, no matter how many players they produce (and the northern American colleges and Olympic teams are producing some fine ones such as Chelios and Carpenter), hockey is *not* in the American blood the way it is for us. The story in *Sports Illustrated* is written on eggshells, as if in fear of making a false move because the writer, as knowledgeable as he is, is not writing from the absolute surety that comes from a ''hands-on'' intuitive sense of what the game of hockey is all about, and of what it means to be a Canadian who has experienced the national metaphor becoming a reality every icy night of his life.

The boys get back on the bus, some staggering though their shopping bags are lighter. The game, players, and fans have never had much class in the big leagues. If you wish to see hockey played in all its glory, return to some familiar small town and seek out the outdoor rinks or frozen ponds; put on your skates and share the joy on the faces of the skaters as they glide up and down on the ice. Listen to the sound.

The City of Vancouver looms ahead, sprawling, disconnected, gorgeous in its mural landscape, yet a city lacking in human compassion. A city of free enterprise but without human dimension, a place where you live by the sword or you don't live. A cold city but not cold enough for hockey, a city that houses a team that used to fly about the league in its own private jet, the only NHL team to do so. This is the luxury of free enterprise but it produces a comfortableness in the players that carries onto the ice. The high salaries and creature comforts have turned out coddled, incubated athletes who think of their talent as a profession rather than an art, and play accordingly. On no team is this more evident than the Vancouver Canucks.

We are die-hard hockey fans on this bus. Who else would travel over seven hours return trip in one day at a cost of $50.00, including ticket, to see a hockey game? We cut through the centre of Vancouver making for the Pacific National Exhibition grounds that lie on the east side. Vancouver is the only hockey town I've been in that doesn't have its shrine in the centre of the city. The sky thickens as we approach the Pacific Coliseum. Rain is always a threat here, even when the sun is out. Vancouverites claim immunity but their feet are webbed.

Hastings and Renfrew. The PNE grounds. The Coliseum looks like a huge grey bowl. The kids are eager to get to the souvenir shop for the mid-season sales. I try to pretend I'm not. The hot chocolate is scalding but necessary, the cashews look like extracted teeth. Nothing has changed. The arena has the same damp smell it has always had.

The first impression of the Pacific Coliseum is one of smallness. It's as if the upper level of the arena has been cut off, leaving only the "reds" and "blues" seating. We take our seats and are made instantly aware of how far we are from the ice: the seats slant upward at less of an angle than at the Gardens in Toronto or the Forum in Montreal. This gives the Coliseum the illusion of space and largeness; the reality is that the fan is further away from the action than in most NHL arenas. As a result, I find that one has the feeling of being dissociated from the play. We are all watchful observers at the Coliseum but it is virtually impossible for the Vancouver fan to feel in the game. The necessary intimacy is lost. This is the reason for ''the wave,'' a desperate attempt by the fans to show that they are still there, that they still matter in arenas that are increasingly designed as ''multi-purpose facilities'' rather than hockey rinks.

It is good to see the familiar Boston black sweaters again. There are living memories of the best of hockey emblazoned on these jerseys. Sinden is behind the bench, Pete Peters in nets, and the team still has the likes of Ray Bourque, Rick Middleton, and Terry O'Reilly out front. The first period is open and good. Play is unusually crisp, the passing excellent. Maybe something of the Russian game has rubbed off on the unit, as a team. The Canucks have the ability to move the puck too but seem to spend most of their ice-time skating against it.

Richard Brodeur is outstanding in nets, but he receives little support from his defence. In a game in which split-second timing is everything, the Canucks always check the man a second too late. They give the appearance of making the extra effort, but it is after the fact and therefore token. They are often too little, and always too late.

The great play of the opening period is made by the Canucks' Peter McNab, the old ex-Bruin, who digs the puck out of the corner and threads a perfect pass to either of two Vancouver forwards parked in front. McNab is often accused of being one of the slowest men in the league, and this may well be so, but he plays with an intelligence that makes him a factor each time he's on the ice. Place him on a line with one or two goal-scorers and he would make a major contribution to the Canucks. But they don't have one or two goal scorers, with the possible exception of Tony Tanti.

Brodeur is particularly fine at playing the angles, a task he does to perfection. He knows just how far to come out so the opposing forward sees only the pads looming like pillars at the entrance to some unattainable fortress. He and McNab must bring a great deal of intelligence and common sense to this team, on and off the ice.

Surprisingly, there is little of the unnecessary, antagonistic roughing and fighting here that one sees so often in junior hockey. What carries on in the NHL however, is the awful habit of stickholding and, in the first period, it almost leads to a serious injury. Stan Smyl and Terry O'Reilly meet at the Boston blueline and O'Reilly grabs Smyl's stick in the now-accustomed illegal fashion: his right hand on his own stick as he follows the play, his left holding Smyl's stick as the scrappy Canuck captain attempts to penetrate the Bruins zone. Smyl twists and yanks his stick twice to free it from O'Reilly's grasp, then jerks his blade upward with renewed vigour a third time, not realizing that O'Reilly has finally let go a moment before. The Bruin player, bent low to push off instantly and get back into the play, receives a bad cut over his left ear that narrowly misses his eye. It would be grotesque to say that this would have been O'Reilly's own fault, but the incident goes to show how serious, stupid, and dangerous this accepted practice has become.

Ken "the Rat" Linseman ties the score in the final minute of the second period, capitalizing on the only weakness Brodeur has — rebounds. Rick Middleton makes a fine play for Boston's second goal by Lukowich in the last minute but Brodeur is given no help on this one. The Vancouver defense deserts him at the worst moments and protects him when he needs help least. Brodeur allows rebounds and the Bruin forwards know it and go for the net where they take turns perching like vultures.

The natural speed and flow of the game is eroded by too much icing and too many TV commercials. Teams used to ice the puck when they were under great pressure *and* a line had been out too long. Now they seem to ice it at the first hint of trouble.

It is not for nothing that Rick Middleton is known around the league as "Nifty." I quickly lost count of how many near-goals he set up with his firm, sure passes, but oohs and aahs followed him whenever he touched the puck. It's been reported he uses copper rivets rather than steel ones to hold his blades to his skate boots because he stops and starts so quickly he places unusual stress on his blades. We certainly saw a great deal of Middleton shifting from one direction to another but it was his intuitive puck sense that so delighted the crowd. Middleton never followed the puck; rather it followed him. He would sweep over the blueline, pass off to one of his wingers, and head for the corner or drift behind the net, entirely out of the play, the puck being held by a group of players halfway up the boards. Again and again the puck would squirt from the scramble of players and head straight for Middleton's stick as if it were a magnet. Alone, with time to dance about on his copper rivets, Nifty would then wheel out of the corner or shift from behind the net like a quarterback choosing between two or three open receivers. The Bruins, long accustomed to the close relationship between Middleton and the puck, would accelerate from the swarm and scramble to all sorts of wide-open ice, huge white free spaces shining with potential success.

Middleton's performance was a thing of beauty. He made the whole tedious trip worthwhile. His intuitive grasp of the game, his weaving moves, his imaginative plays and perfect passes thrilled those in attendance. That Sunday, Nifty and the Bruins were a vivid illustration of what the game can be. It was the kind of performance that stays well beyond the TV cameras, and well beyond the jaded, unsophisticated sensibility of most sports journalists, but 15,000 Vancouverites were treated to a rare display of excellence that night, one that they are not likely to forget for many games to come.

''The Steamer'' sends the game into overtime with his nineteenth goal of the year at 15:51 and Thomas Gradin, whom we have not seen all game, wins it with his twentieth at the 26-second mark of overtime but we Island fans can only hear the cheering. Ordered back to our bus by a certain time designed to catch the last ferry back to Victoria, we just settle in and begin to pull away when Gradin pots the winner.

The next day I devour the wire service report of the game. The article reads like the box score: not a single element of the contest is discussed that is not immediately apparent in the conventional summary. In fact the box score, giving a chronological account of the goals, assists, penalties, shots on goal, the referee and the attendance, is much more informative than the press report.

Who filed such a report? Could it really have been written by a human? There is no life to the writing, no discussion of the finer points of the game that were continuously on view, no appreciation of the art that 15,000 of us experienced. The skating was exciting, the speed of the game and the pinpoint passing were wonderful to behold. Other highlights? The way the Bruins swept up-ice and regrouped as a team, rather than a bunch of individuals. There was method to their wonderful madness and it was a joy to behold. And the Vancouver crowd appreciated the fine play, punctuating their cheers for the home team with frequent oohs and aahs at the Bruins' artistry. I don't recall the three stars of the game but they must have been chosen by the guy who wrote the newspaper story. Rick Middleton, the finest player on the ice that night, wasn't among them.

Superstition:
An Edge on the Game

It is unlucky to be behind at the end of the game.
> — former basketball star, Bill Russell

Everyone is superstitious when frightened.
> — Northrop Frye

The smell of wintergreen stings the nostrils upon entering the dressing-room. The equipment bag slumps to the concrete floor and a foul-smelling sweatshirt falls out. It is the smell of victory, the sacred sweatshirt not to be laundered until the streak is broken.

Gretzky always keeps the left side of his sweater tucked into his pants. It looks disheveled, sloppy, untidy. It is. More importantly, it is part of the same routine he has followed since he was five, when he played with boys twice his age and his sweater was much too big for him. That's the practical reason. It fails to explain why he also has to be first on the ice at the beginning of every game and indeed, at the start of each period.

91

Like most players, he is also superstitious about his number. There is little need to explain why Gretzky uses black tape on his stick or pours baby powder over his stick-blade. There are practical reasons — black tape keeps the puck from spinning, baby powder prevents the snow on the ice from sticking. But these habits are also superstitions. He does them because they worked, once.

It is the only common thing about Wayne Gretzky. Most hockey players — though few will admit it — are superstitious. Some are more elaborate in their ritual than others. Sometimes a player's particular superstitions become part of the team's general routine, such as whacking the goalie's pads, tapping the posts like Ron Hextall, or patting a teammate's bum as he passes by.

During the 1984 federal election, Liberal leader John Turner got himself in hot water by routinely patting the behinds of several Liberal candidates, most noticeably that of Iona Campagnola. While no single gaffe cost Mr Turner the election, this particular one caused considerable turmoil in the Liberal camp for several weeks. No one in the Liberal party seems to have understood Turner's entirely innocent gesture, which comes from the world of sports. Turner's conception of a political party as a team undergoing a grueling playoff was hardly new or news, but his ritual bum-patting encouragement of his ''players'' was completely misunderstood by a country that takes pride in its knowledge of sports. On a team the camaraderie that is developed from such ritual is akin to a group of voyageurs sitting around a campfire. In the same fashion, a hockey team skates in circles against the evil eye of the night.

The superstitions of Phil Esposito are legendary. Like most hockey players, ''Espo'' prepared for every game the

same way. While the streak was on, he wore the same tie and drove the same route to each game.

Most hockey players have pre-game rituals. Some put their sweaters on a certain way, some lay out their gear in a particular order, others put it on the same way each time, the cup inside or out, left side or right side first, depending on what was successful the last time out. One of my nephews puts a penny in his jock for good luck. During practise, he wears odd socks. He always goes to the arena 30 minutes before the start of the game, regardless of what his coach dictates. Off the ice, he even keeps his team's pennant with his girlfriend's name embossed on it in his bedroom.

Coaches also have their rituals — wearing the same "winning" outfit to the rink, or carrying the same objects to the bench before each period. Most coaches prefer to keep their rituals private, and would choose to carry something innocuous such as a first aid kit or a pail of pucks. "Red" Kelly was an exception. When he coached the Leafs he was famous for his superstitions, the most noted being his belief in "pyramid power," the rays of positive power that emanate from the pyramid. Kelly had a series of small pyramids placed under the Leaf bench during playoff games that year. Judging from the outcome of the playoff, the positive rays were absorbed by others in the building.

Some superstitions begin spontaneously, but most have a long-forgotten tradition behind them. The more important the game, the more a player or coach is going to call on the gods to grant the sweet smell of champagne in the dressing-room. During the '50s and '60s the Montreal Canadiens developed superstition and ritual into a high art. Claude Provost was the chief protagonist. "Old Lantern Jaw" would cross himself each time just before touching the ice, while several other players could be seen mouthing a Hail Mary or the occasional Lord's Prayer before the start of the game. And who can forget the Flyers of the mid-1970s who employed Kate Smith singing God Bless America to launch them on the warpath? Goalies are particularly haunting, especially Philadelphia's Ron Hextall. Of all current NHLers, Hextall has the most publicized sequence of rituals, which includes charging the opposition bench during the pre-game warmups, banging his stick on the boards, and challenging the players and coach.

Part of my own ritual was getting dressed the same way — and the right way — every time. Jockstrap, garterbelt, socks to the bottom on both sides, shin pads in, then bring the socks up, with the skates loose and shuffle everything into a form-feeling position. As if I was going to the grave. And I'd tape the stuff in but the skates were still open, then tie them as loose as possible with maximum support (the feeling of freedom within the skate), and I don't bring the skate up to me, I always tie it on the floor. One final tie, always finishing with the right skate, but I never wrap the laces around the ankle. Then, the pants, standing up, adjust the jock. This is the ritual of the dressing-room. The pants don't fit on you, they hang, they have to float. The strap of the pants must go under the shoulder pads. Then, shoulder pads, elbow pads, sweater, in no particular order. And then I would pray that I and my team would play well — it was not somehow considered fair to ask for more — and that no one would get hurt. After that it was every man for himself. Whatever happened, happened. The game was in the hands of the gods.

My older brother recalls: "If you won you didn't touch anything. If your mother came near your stuff to wash it you shouted: 'Don't touch that!' You didn't wash anything, or ever switch your stick, or change the tape. On the bench, as a defenceman, you always took the outside seat, your defence partner on the inside. Unlike baseball, hockey doesn't allow you to think about superstition — you just did it.''

Both as an international and national attention-getter, the government officials and bureaucrats responsible for Expo '86 in Vancouver initially dreamed up the idea of symbolizing Canada's hosting of the World's Fair with a pair of giant crossed hockey sticks as the national emblem or symbolic arches through which visitors to the fair would walk. There were obviously no former hockey players on the board of directors of the World Exposition. Hockey players have an immediate and deeply-felt uneasiness about the skull and cross-bones of crossed hockey sticks and avoid them whenever they can. Crossed hockey sticks mean one thing and one thing only: someone is going to get hurt. Hockey sticks crossed bring only injury. They are a symbolic manifestation of death. The sticks merged into a single blade with puck before the fair opened.

There is no question that superstition gives a hockey player increased confidence. But there is more to it than that.

The game is played on solid ice with sharp blades and sharpened sticks at speeds of up to 30 miles an hour in a confined space. It is a dangerous game. The hockey player needs something more than physical protection. The goaltender, defenceman, and particularly the forward are often performing literally out-of-control. This is one of the chief attractions of the game, but it also gives the athlete limited control over the contest, not to mention himself. In a secular age in which we pride ourselves on being able to take full control of our lives, the game of hockey harkens back to an earlier ancestral time when fate or chance, as exemplified by a rolling puck, a missed open net, or a freak injury, could determine the outcome of a game or even the direction of one's life. Though we now find superstitions quaint and amusing, if the gods do continue to live, the superstitious athlete believes that he or she may be able to gain a slight edge on the game by the evocation of luck to help in the control of such uncertainties. The pre-game '87 playoff brawl between the Flyers and Canadiens attests to the importance of ritual and superstition. Both teams were trying to get ''an edge on the game.''

Playing the role of the dull matter-of-fact Canadians we pretend to be, we hate to admit that superstition plays a part in our national consciousness. Repressed in most areas of our daily life, superstition reveals itself more fully in the game of hockey. There — though we may suspect that such attention might bring us misfortune — we allow ourselves to be placed in the hands of the gods.

Wayne Gretzky:
The Difference Between Us

In front of excellence,
the immortal gods have put sweat,
and long and steep is the way to it.
                    — Hesiod, c. 700 B.C.
Gretzky is like an invisible man. He appears out of nowhere,
passes to nowhere, and a goal is scored.
                    — **Soviet assistant coach, Ivan Dmitriev**

At some time in his early youth, a young boy growing up in Canada has one burning desire: to play "the game" well and make the NHL. This desire, found in every region of the country, is what makes Canadians — and particularly Canadiens — burn.

In Canada, hockey has never been a luxury, something that one idles with in one's spare time — even when one is doing just that. Canadian boys are born with the dream, and have the will to reach for the brass ring, the black puck. "It's every boy's dream to play in the NHL and I'm living out my dream," said Luc Robitaille, soon after he joined the Los Angeles Kings.

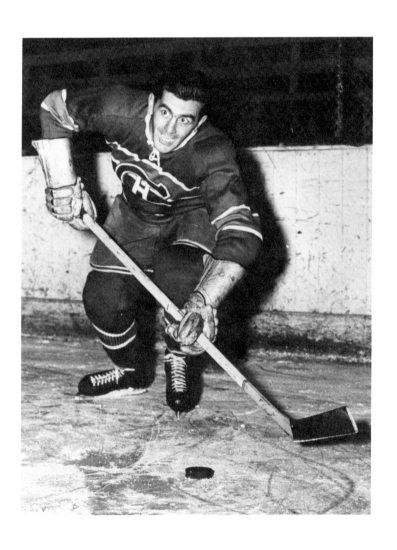

But the question has to be asked, and answered: what are the elements that go into making the difference between a star player and a journeyman, one who is merely good? What motivates the star athlete? What gives him the desire and dedication to excel? What are the magic ingredients?

Well, they may not be magical but they certainly are psychological. They often make the difference between us mortals and a playoff hero.

Dedication is a word that often comes to mind when hockey enthusiasts discuss the difference between a good player and one who excels at the game. Excellence stems from the Latin word *excelere*, "to outrun others." Interviewed by Murray Malkin in the *Globe and Mail*, Yvan Cournoyer, known as the "Road Runner" for his blinding speed, said: "When I was a youngster my whole life was dedicated to hockey. When I played other sports ... it was because I wanted to stay in shape for hockey. When I delivered beer for Labatts for three summers I knew it would make me strong for hockey. And as a child I also knew that scraping the ice and pushing the snow would give me strong legs.... On the Canadiens, we couldn't lose because for us that was against the law."

Attitude is the major ingredient in a player's make-up and it is the one thing impossible to measure. It cannot be found or ferreted out, only guessed at by scout, general manager, or coach. If only managers and coaches could read the minds of their players. The Russian goaltender Tretiak has spoken of winning games 17-0 and being dissatisfied with his and his team's performance, feeling that they had not played the game the way it could be played, despite the score.

"They had three chances to score in the second (period)," said Team NHL coach Jean Perron, "and they scored on all three." Of course they did. They expected to. Obviously, "they" must be the Russian national hockey team. Journeyman players in the NHL would not have that positive an attitude. Not in a league where it's good enough to simply hurl the puck in the general direction of the net, take 40 or more shots a game, and hope that the law of averages will let a couple in.

Jari Kurri, Finnish master of the "one-timer" has one of the highest shooting percentages in the NHL. His success is not only based upon his ability to quick-release, or his good fortune in playing on Gretzky's line. Kurri expects to score every time he shoots. He has been called a natural goal scorer blessed with a scorer's hands. But it is Kurri's winning attitude that has netted him an amazing 354 goals in just seven NHL seasons. Every time he shoots, Kurri expects to score and appears genuinely baffled and disappointed when he doesn't.

Most difficult of all is to maintain a positive attitude when the odds are against you. The man to whom this book is dedicated was a master at "playing against the odds." John Atkinson always made certain he was on the team that had fewer players. Often, in shinny, we'd end up with 9, 11, or 13 playing and John was always on the team with the lesser number. On several occasions I noticed that when we had an even number of players on the ice warming up, John would try to make up teams that would pit four against six, five against seven, or six against eight. He was always on the smaller squad, valiantly struggling against the odds. It was a no-lose situation, a strategy he carried over into his daily life. Even at the time, I felt there was something odd about this behavior — something oddly Canadian.

John's unorthodox approach pulled me through more than once. I vividly remember sitting in the dressing room on a skate-scarred wooden bench between the second and third periods of a midget playoff game. We were down 3-1 and my teammates and I had been floating all game. Suddenly I said to myself: ''Look — I'm a failure in high school. I don't have a girlfriend. I stutter. I'm a shy, pimply-faced kid, but I'm the guy who's gonna turn this game around. I'm the guy who has the desire and imagination to take control of this game and win the thing for my team and be a hero.'' I scored two goals and we won 6-4. I could feel that mysterious moment when the goddess Nike turned the battle into victory.

Self-confidence is vital, the feeling that you are able to do just about anything on the ice. It's as if you're in complete command. Look at a Mark Howe as he moves up the ice dictating the play, like Doug Harvey did for so many years with the Canadiens. Or Glenn Anderson bursting through the Flyer defence. As Grant Fuhr says, ''You can't doubt yourself. If you doubt yourself, you lose.''

As well as the basic principles of his craft, the star player has a spontaneity that borders on carelessness. Every team has a couple of guys who play the game at a higher level. I think here particularly of Mark Messier of the Oilers. Messier plays imaginatively, seizes opportunities, looks for openings, does things you would not expect a player to do, like taking a shot on the short side when it looks to be covered, or cutting to the net when it seems impossible to make it.

And the star athlete is able to play at the height of his game and beyond, year after year. Consistency is one of the key differences between the star and the average talent, but this quality is often underrated by NHL management. NHL scouting reports had No. 1 prospect Pierre Turgeon as being ''inconsistent and an underachiever.'' An early choice, Dave Archibald, was criticized ''for lacking intensity and not performing in important matches.'' Said one scout: ''When his team needs him in big games, Archibald doesn't seem to be around. In an 11-5 game he racks up points, but too often you don't see him when the score's 3-2.'' In contrast, Brendan Shanahan was described as a ''character player and team leader.'' But Shanahan was not drafted first. Statistics speak louder than a player's attitude. But the great players are always consistent. Trottier. Kerr. Middleton. Lowe. Lemieux. Hawerchuk.

The foregoing qualities necessitate a drive, emotional energy, and a strong personality that clearly separates the men from the boys. Essential, too, is the psychological trait that makes defeat ''not only inconceivable but intolerable'' according to former New York Islander Bob Nystrom. As he puts it: ''More than anything else you need the burning desire to win and a mental toughness.'' Courage, concentration, pride, and more than a little ruthlessness are also fundamental in the make-up of a star. In the great performer, the psychological traits combine and call forth a more elusive one called ''hockey sense.''

Great players may have their genesis here — young players adopt the mannerisms of their personal heroes, emulate their style, and move unconsciously into their own hockey sense. One way to play the game well is to pretend that you are Teeder Kennedy or Tod Sloan, Hull, Orr, Nesterenko, Gretzky; whoever has caught your fancy because of his style of play. Whoever you play against is disadvantaged if he isn't pretending to be anybody but himself. It is not that he is limited in what he can do; it is simply that he is playing against two — one a boy his age, the ''other'' an NHL star. This fantasizing about stardom and becoming the other player is common among those who've played the game since childhood.

My hockey hero was Ted ''Teeder'' Kennedy, the heart

and soul of the Leafs for over a decade. In 12 years Teeder played on five Stanley Cup champions, scoring 231 goals. But it was as a team leader that captain Kennedy played a most important role. Some call it heart, others guts, some drive ... but it all boils down to hockey sense.

Hockey sense is knowing where the puck or teammate will be, without looking; hockey sense is also how you wear your equipment, how you carry your stick (you always keep it blade down when you're on the bench), how you present yourself. It's how you tape your stick, the way a sweater is worn, a natural feeling for the game on and off the ice, as well as being in position at the right time. It's not something that can be taught. Some have it, some don't. It is an instinct with the best players.

Wayne Gretzky synthesizes all of the above qualities, but it is his imaginative and loving approach to hockey that makes the difference. Gretzky has said that he never considers practise, practise; "it (is always) fun ... I love the game so much and I've never stopped loving it. But I could play Tuesday and Friday hockey with 15 or 20 friends and enjoy it just as much."

In a *Time* magazine cover story of March 1985, The Great One likened the NHL to "a university" and called hockey "the study of geometry ... angles and caroms." Gretzky's ability to see the game several moves ahead of the action is akin to a Grand Master of chess who sees both where the chess pieces are and where they will be. As Mario Lemieux once said, "Before I get the puck I look where the players are and try to determine where they will be after .... It's easy."

Athletes like Gretzky "can translate their ideal or goal into an actual physical vision," observes Bryan Smith, an organizational consultant with Jackson Smith Ltd., in Toronto.

They can "see it, taste it, smell it, and imagine the sounds and emotions associated with it." This mental imagery, known as "visualization," has been employed by West Coast shamans and other religious mystics for centuries.

There is no doubt. Wayne Gretzky is the finest hockey player in the game today and one of the greatest players who has ever played the game. No other player today best combines all the skills the game demands. It is this synthesis of skills — and his creative imaginative approach — rather than any single attribute that has earned Gretzky the accolade of the game's greatest player. Such an honour is awarded by one's peers; it cannot be asked for. One is chosen because he embodies the best attributes of the Canadian spirit on ice. In this respect Gretzky follows in the hallowed tradition of Aurel Joliat, Newsy Lalonde, Howie Morenz, Richard, Howe, Hull, and Orr; all hockey immortals.

There is no better way to grasp Gretzky's achievement than to look at a single statistic: The Great One got his 1,000th point in a little more than five seasons. The first 17 players who reached that milestone — and most don't — took an average of 16 ½ seasons. Another comparison? Gordie Howe scored a lifetime total of 1,850 points. It took Howe 26 seasons. Currently, Gretzky, fourth on the list of all-time leading scorers, has over 1,500 points in 8 years in the league. Goals? Gretzky scored 525 goals in his first 600 games. Guy Lafleur experienced his "little death" or retirement at 518; the great Jean Beliveau had 507 when he hung up the blades. Yet the game has had great players throughout its long history. In 1910, Newsy Lalonde led the league in scoring with 38 goals. In 11 games. In 1917, in the first season of the NHL, Joe Malone scored 44 goals in half as many games, a feat never equalled.

What is it about hockey players that makes them the only ones eligible for national worship? Why do we have so few heroes in this country, unlike America, where every president creates his own deity by right of office? Why aren't our prime ministers held in high esteem in the national consciousness? There is even a lack of heroes in Canadian history. As much as historians have tried to elevate Louis Riel into a politico-mythological deity, people are still confused about Riel's role: he as easily represents Canadian separatism as Canadian nationalism. A mythological hero must have mythological versatility, but his ultimate role cannot lead to confusion in the minds of his worshippers. As well, Riel represents the losing side of the Canadian psyche. Who do so few of our pioneers, politicians, artists, entrepreneurs — even our world-class athletes — stir the national imagination?

Because hockey is the closest thing to our hearts. Our heroes must come from ''the game'' that means so much to us as Canadians. Our hockey heroes are instantly recognizable. Gretzky, Orr, Howe, Lanny McDonald and others are mobbed everywhere they go. Laurie Graham, Ken Read, Todd Brooker, and Steve Podborski are celebrities in Europe; in Canada they are honoured but they are not gods. If they walked down the street, almost no one would recognize them. In contrast, a Gretzky or Howe is surrounded minutes after entering a restaurant.

Even Ben Johnson, the world's fastest man, fails to capture our collective imagination. But the Rocket, refereeing for the travelling NHL oldtimers, is mobbed by 50 or 60 kids when he arrives at his hotel— kids who were not even born when he played. The Rocket feigns embarrassment. There are no other oldtimers around. ''Ou sont les gars?'' asks Richard. Finally Norm Ullman comes out of the hotel. ''Es-tu fatigue,́

Norm?'' asks the Rocket. But he knows the answer. The other guys are not tired; they are not the Rocket. They are not legends. Only the Rocket is a god.

It is the most natural thing in the world to want heroes, men and women who embody the national consciousness. But, paradoxically, Canadians are not comfortable with heroic figures. We are a people capable of ''rebounding'' on our heroes, of turning a hero into a wimp in a moment's notice. We more easily worship mediocrity. Gretzky is too good. We have no measurement for him; we want to bring him down to our size. We tell ourselves he's a wimp: he often gets booed around the league; we complain he whines to referees (but he *is*, after all, the captain); we accuse him of taking dives; he refuses to fight.

We don't like our own, especially when they're winners. Success does not rest easily on our shoulders. Oiler coach Glen Sather has suggested that many Edmonton citizens resent the team for their success. Nevertheless, a country requires individual archetypes and, in this regard, Wayne Gretzky is the archetypal Canadian hero — small, self-effacing — and incomparably great. Because hockey so clearly defines the Canadian experience, Wayne Gretzky is the latest in a long line of hockey heroes who personify the hopes, wishes, and dreams of the Canadian people.

The hero has the ability to make us feel we live a larger life. He gives our lives significance, connects us to the great possibilities that lie within us, to the hope that we could be the exception. How beautifully Gretzky articulates the average Canadian's hopes and aspirations. On a team laden with outstanding talent, Gretzky is not the fastest skater, best face-off man, or the strongest. His basic skills are no better than several other star players. Yet, each season he's 50 to 80 points ahead of his peers. He reminds us that the fantasies of the average Canadian fan have a chance to be real.

Both on and off the ice, Gretzky embodies both of our national games — hockey and the business of making money. To be a true-blue Canadian hero, one must be successful in business terms. There is no room for the politician or artist here, or for the Louis Riels of our society, for money is the measure of the Canadian, our crowning glory. One must want to emulate the hero who most distinctly expresses the central values of the culture and who clearly demonstrates the ability to overcome the fears and nightmares of the ice-cold Canadian experience. As Al Purdy put it in ''Homage to Ree-shard,'' ''... they came each spring showering ice cream and chocolate bars on all the kids in my home town, they were the new gods almost replacing money...''.

Gretzky is not simply speaking to us of the game; it's deeper than that and we know it. Privately we acknowledge — and indeed honour — his business successes, but we don't like to admit it to ourselves, out loud, unlike Americans, who are not bothered by flamboyance. Only the hockey star combines both elements of the Canadian heroic mold.

Gretzky is the quintessential Canadian hero who, on black skates in lieu of a white horse, transforms the common Canadian experience of struggle, hardship, and survival, into grace, then beauty, and finally, mastery over the forces of nature in our country on ice.

In shining armour he skates forth from the unconscious factors of our communal or social existence, playing a game that is the perfect Canadian compromise between collective effort and individual striving. Despite the near-heroic achievements of the Toronto Blue Jays the past few years, no single player has gained the hero-worship of the fans and national media. A baseball player, boxer, or tennis star cannot hope to embody the Canadian experience because these sports do not speak to the sense of darkness, cold, and terror of the great white unknown that Canadians unconsciously feel. Only hockey expresses the Canadian psyche and experience, and only hockey is at the omphalos or midpoint of our world. This is the true significance of Wayne Gretzky. By finding greatness in him, we find it in ourselves.

The Artemis Factor: Women in Hockey

Aggression? It's just yourself coming out, totally unfiltered.
Hockey is a kind of spiritual growth — a direct route.

— **Katherine Chapman**

Your mom *plays* HOCKEY*!?*

— **a friend of Katherine Chapman's son**

In 1985, 12-year-old Justine Blainey lost her court battle to join an all-boys Metro-Toronto Hockey League team. Justine is but one of approximately 27,000 girls and young women currently playing Canada's unofficial national sport. Justine wanted to be one of the 175,000 players in the Metro-Toronto League, but she was barred because of a league rule prohibiting females. In team tryouts she placed 14th among 64 players. Hockey teams carry 20 players each. Justine had made the team. But she hadn't. Justine is a girl.

Why does she want to play the game? ''I love it when you hit somebody,'' Justine says.

The Ontario Human Rights Code permits sex discrimination in athletics. While this would appear to violate the

Canadian Charter of Rights and Freedoms, the Supreme Court of Ontario ruled that the violation was reasonable. Mr Justice Donald Steele based his decision on an override section in the Charter that says though a law may violate the Charter, it is still valid if it can be shown to be ''demonstrably justified in a free and democratic society.'' For ''demonstrably justified,'' read ''traditional and masculine.'' Bruce Kidd, sports historian and professor at the University of Toronto, feels the Ontario court decision ''allows men to keep unexamined their very deep fears of playing with and against females.'' Two years later, in 1987, Justine was presenting her case again — this time before the Ontario Human Rights Commission. The attorney general of Ontario has pledged to repeal the contentious section of the Human Rights Code, but this will take time. It may come too late for Justine Blainey.

(It is interesting to note that Justine's application was opposed by the Canadian Amateur Hockey Association, the Ontario Hockey Association, *and* the Ontario Women's Hockey Association. This last organization is concerned that men would want to join women's teams if Justine had been granted the right to play on a boys' team. However, according to *Globe and Mail* reporter Kirk Makin, men have not ''rushed to join women's teams in other provinces where they are allowed to do so.'')

Abby Hoffman, now director of Sport Canada, remembers her own attempt to play in a boys' league some 30 years ago: ''The game was fast and a lot of fun and exciting and all of those things. I wasn't conscious of the fact there weren't any girls playing. Adults are aware of those things. Kids just want to play.''

In some parts of Canada, however, things are beginning to change in organized hockey. The Manitoba Amateur Association once barred a 13-year-old, Julie Milne of Letellier, from playing with a local Pee Wee team. Now, however, the MAA has a policy giving girls the same access as boys to facilities and playing time. And, "where no separate but equal program exists, any female may register and play integrated hockey in her respective category or division," according to Bev Gaidosch, the MAA's director of women's hockey. The MAA has decided that any girls who qualify to play on a boys' team — where there is no comparable girls' league — will be able to get changed in the locker room, the washroom, or come to the rink ready to play.

Most officials who make policy about girls' participation in organized hockey will agree that pre-pubescent girls compete favourably with boys. In fact, girls at that age are often more coordinated, stronger, and more skilled. After puberty, however, boys grow at a faster rate. They become taller, stronger, heavier — ergo, the contest becomes "unfair." But the policy-makers forget that the true skills of a hockey player have nothing to do with size. The superb player excels at skating, stickhandling, puck-handling, finesse, inventiveness, imagination, and checking. There is no reason why a young woman would be disadvantaged at any of these. The fact that someone is bigger than you does not make him (or her) a better checker. When I played, some of the biggest guys I played against were the easiest to avoid because they were slow, awkward skaters. Some of the hardest and best body-checkers are the smaller guys, like Stan Smyl of the Vancouver Canucks. When we say that a player "really knows how to throw his weight around," we are not saying anything about how much "he" weighs — we are talking about the ability to give (and take) a solid bodycheck. Just as it doesn't hurt to hit the ice or the boards (if you know how to do it), so it does not hurt to get checked by someone twice your size. In fact, it can be fun. Justine Blainey knows this. Anyone who has played the game knows it too.

Twenty-six-year-old Becky Smith of Cape Breton got her first hockey stick four days before her first birthday. She remembers staring at the back of cereal boxes as a girl, reading about the NHL stars of the '60s as she ate breakfast. Bobby Rousseau was her favourite. Becky also remembers staying up late to watch Hockey Night in Canada with her father. ''I don't know why the inclination to play the game was there,'' she says, ''but it was. We had a coke driveway and I'd be out there for hours on end bashing away at the coke with my little hockey stick. I was always by myself, playing alone.

''Two years later we moved to a new housing division where there were 103 kids, or some such outrageous number, from 40 houses. We all played street hockey. Girls and boys — together. All ages. I remember a guy named Michael Fargo who was 11 or 12 years old. The rest of us were six or seven. Of course he was much bigger but he insisted on playing with the little kids. He used to slash at our ankles when we came in on net. I got carried home on the shoulders of the rest of the kids one day because I was the only one who bomped him back after he took out three kids in a row.

''I got into league play in 1972 in Charlottetown. This was shinny on ice and strictly for girls. We played with a street hockey ball, helmet, gloves, skates, and shin pads if you wanted them. It didn't matter what kind of skates you wore, figure skates or hockey skates. From there we evolved into a duplicate of a boys' minor hockey league.

''The only alteration in the game for girls is in the shoulder pads, which are like the old defenceman's pads —

longer in the front pecs and down almost to the bottom of the rib cage. We wear those with two hard cups on the front. And instead of a jock, there's a ''jill.'' It's a latex rubber-coated triangle worn the same way as a jock except it doesn't travel underneath quite so far. They're also used in girls' lacrosse.

''I don't play regularly now, but I still love the game. Recently I played goal for a non-contact recreation league, men and women, ages 18 to 45. Their goalie didn't show up so I stepped between the pipes. I know that my defence was doing a little more than the average clearing and checking in front to make sure I had a clear view, but there were slapshots and I was able to handle everything.''

Becky Smith is convinced women will play in the National Hockey League before the turn of the century. But this will happen only when minor hockey associations stop segregating girls after the bantam level age of 13-14.

Bruce Kidd agrees with Smith. During his testimony at Justine Blainey's 1987 hearing, he pointed out that no one knows what kind of performance women are really capable of. Women in the past have been restrained by social convention, by open ridicule, and by lack of opportunity. But now, says Kidd, ''Women are achieving performances that nobody dreamed possible.'' He reminded the Ontario Human Rights Commission that blacks were kept out of organized baseball in the 1940s by some of the same arguments now being used to bar women from hockey. But Kidd has faith that change is possible. He predicted that women might be playing in the NHL ''within 20 to 50 years,'' and urged that ''outstanding females should be given the opportunity to move onto all-male teams.''

Recreational leagues all over Canada now include talented women players who — like Becky Smith — have always worn black skates. Many are formidable and surprising opponents. Bart Nawinski from Timmins recalls playing defence one night in a beer league. "One of their wingers was a *real* smooth skater. He kept squeezing by me all night, and finally set up their winning goal. When it was over, he skated up to our centre, gave him a big hug, and kissed him — a real long one. It turned out the great winger was our centre's bride-to-be."

But what of the women who predate the sexual emancipation — incomplete as it is — that Becky Smith and Justine Blainey have grown up with? It is a testament to the attraction of the game, to the stirring of hockey in the national spirit, that grown women are trading their white skates for black in ever-increasing numbers. "Most of the players on our team are over 30," explains Brenda Herbison of Argenta, BC. "When we play other women's teams, they skate circles around us. They're all 14 to 25 years old and they've played hockey since they were little. We haven't won a game yet."

In the face of such a dismal record, why does Herbison drive almost two hours round trip twice a week to hockey practise in Kaslo? "It's good for my character," she says. "There's something therapeutic about asserting myself this way. To take the puck and skate down the ice with it, you have to have a certain confidence." Unlike Blainey, however, Herbison does *not* "love it" when she hits someone. "I'd quit straightaway if there was heavy bodychecking. It wouldn't be like an art any more. It would put me right off." Herbison's team plays against a local rep team of 10-year-old boys and she says they're "well disciplined and very polite — and they skunk us every time."

When Katherine Chapman was growing up in Calgary,

she wanted to play hockey "but girls weren't allowed to then. My parents wouldn't let me have a hockey stick." Chapman, now a mother of three, finally got her skates and her stick when she was 27. "Playing hockey — it's the greatest way to learn how to skate. You get that hockey stick in your hand and you don't think about anything else."

Chapman thrives on the intense concentration, and the aggression doesn't bother her. "It's just yourself coming out, totally unfiltered. Hockey is a kind of spiritual growth — a direct route." Chapman even sports a hockey injury — torn shoulder ligaments. "It gets in the way of my cello playing, but I'm serious about hockey. I'm not going to quit over a little thing like that."

With two sons in local leagues, Chapman drives to the arena five times a week. "We're all into hockey, but the difference is that in the summer the boys are out in the barn practising wrist shots and slap shots while I'm working in the garden." (Her older son, Nick, returned from hockey camp to report the other players' amazement: "Your *mom* plays *hockey?!*")

Becoming players has led both Brenda Herbison and Katherine Chapman into the role of hockey fan as well. Herbison admits she watches "a little" and enjoys it much more now that she plays. Chapman is a genuine devotee. "When we first got married, Stan watched hockey all the time. It drove me crazy. But now that I play the game too, I *love* it."

But you don't have to be a player to be a fan. Joyce Gutensohn grew up with televised hockey. "Every Saturday night my parents would sit in the living-room and watch the game. My brother and I had the rest of the house to ourselves. We'd turn off all the lights, put blankets over the dining-room table, and play wild animals.

120

"When we got a little older, my brother started playing on a local team, and on Saturday nights we'd join our parents in the living-room. We knew all the players on all the teams and everybody in the family had their favourites.

"Years later, after I moved away from home, I remember feeling bored and lonely one Saturday night. I didn't know what to do, so I flipped on the TV. There was Hockey Night in Canada with Danny Gallivan. I felt better right away.

"I still follow the game. It's one of those stable, soothing parts of my life, like going home and seeing the furniture I grew up with. It's there, it's supposed to be there, it'll always be there. It's very comforting."

During the hockey season, Claire Johnson of Montreal gets up every day at 6 a.m. to drive her oldest son downtown to the university arena for a 7 a.m. practise. In a typical day, she takes the same son to a nearby suburb for an early evening game. After that game, without taking his stuff off, her son slips into the car and she drives him to a 10 p.m. game in the local town league. While he's playing that game, Claire drives to another suburban rink to pick up her second son, takes him home, then returns to the local arena lot where she leaves the car for her first-born. After trudging home through the snow, she makes hot chocolate and waits for the older boy to come in 'round midnight. Difficult to follow? It is for her, too. If she can, she likes to get the games and practises of her youngest son into her transportation schedule as well. And she also saves time to be with her daughter and her husband. (He plays in an oldtimer's league.)

"You have to have tremendous co-operation between the parents in order to do this," says Johnson. One time, her husband got off the plane after a business trip to Africa and arrived home to find an SOS from Claire pinned to the door. Could he come to the local arena to fill in for a coach who couldn't make the game? Without changing his clothes, he dashed to the rink to relieve his wife behind the bench. Another time, she took to the ice herself to supervise a practise session — when she was seven months pregnant.

"The last time we moved," says Johnson, "we turned down several nice houses we looked at because the basements weren't right. We require a large furnace area with concrete walls and floor so there's space to play shinny and take shots."

It sounds like the hockey mother's job is to drive everywhere and see as many games as possible. But there is a more important role. "Kids use their mother as a target for their tensions and frustrations, even down to criticizing her driving on the way to the game," according to Johnson. "How many times have I thought — if only we can get through this night, this game.... " Each of her sons in turn has been through a phase where he tries to provoke his mother. He spars with her all the way to the rink. The edge and increasing tension is just what he needs out on the ice, and this is the way he psyches himself up for the game. It's a kind of inner stimulus he needs in order to play well, and the player's mother just has to bear it with tact and understanding. Johnson has only one goal: "If we're still friends at the end of the season ... that's the most important thing."

The "Real" National Game

At the time of Confederation there were 80 teams in the country. That same year, the first sports-governing body in North America held their convention in Kingston, Ontario.

Today there are seven orange circles, at centre, in the face-off areas, and around the nets. The game is played in three periods, each of 20 minutes stop time. They play six a side, and the players are fully protected from the waist up. All wear helmets; most sport face masks or cages. There are numerous illegal manoeuvers but few penalties. It is a no-holds-barred release of all the pent-up energies a cold country can possibly repress. It is Canada's official national game. It's called lacrosse.

The indoor variety is far more popular in Canada, where the hockey rink becomes "the box" and the grey cement is hard as ice. The goals are four feet wide, the crossbar four feet from the cold floor. It is the oldest team sport in North America but its origins go back beyond the white man's brief tenure on this continent. The game the French explorers called lacrosse because the stick resembled a bishop's crosier or "hoquet" was originally a Mohawk Indian event of religious significance called ''baggataway.'' Sometimes there were 200 men on one side and the playing field stretched beyond the horizon. According to hockey historian Bill Eskenazi, this deadly form of field hockey was called ''ho-ghee,'' a word players shouted when clubbed over the head with a stick.

Modern lacrosse has taken from several games and other sports have borrowed heavily from lacrosse. Indeed the game most resembles basketball in its use of the 30-second shot rule — a team must take a shot on goal in 30 seconds or give up the ball — and in the passing plays designed to get into position for a good shot on net. Occasionally, lacrosse resembles soccer in the slow control a team may exert, (though, mercifully, there is that half-minute time rule) and the centre area of ''the box'' is very small, a matter of a few yards. There is little or no middle ground in lacrosse (this in a country that has become famous throughout the world for staking out that particular territory).

New Westminster, British Columbia, is the Montreal or sacred city of lacrosse and Kevin Alexander of Victoria is the Wayne Gretzky of the indoor game. In fact several NHL players were stars in BC lacrosse, the most notable being John Ferguson, Tom McVie, former coach of the Winnipeg Jets, and Jack Bioda, former Boston Bruin defenceman.

Today it seems that hockey has somehow evolved backward in time to incorporate many of the more violent tendencies of its brother sport. Today's hockey more closely resembles its ancient counterpart than at any other time, with its adaptation of helmets, face guards or visors, and its cacophonic symphony of slashing, hooking, cross-checking, holding, tripping, boarding, butt-ending or spearing, charging, checking from behind, blind-siding, elbowing, fighting, high-sticking, interfering, kneeing, and unnecessary roughness and goon tactics. In the ancient days of lacrosse, games often ended only when a player on one side or the other died.

The West Coast Connection

Every Canadian city, town, and village has a hockey history. Even a city as small and wet as Victoria, BC has a great hockey tradition to draw on. Currently, the city is the home of the Victoria Cougars, a junior A hockey club which has been the training ground in recent years for such NHL stalwarts as Grant Fuhr, Mel Bridgman, Barry Pederson, Geoff and Russ Courtnall, Paul Cyr, Bob McGill, Curt Fraser, Greg Adams, and Murray Bannerman. Yet few fans realize that the Victoria Cougars won the Stanley Cup in 1925 and were in the cup final 11 years earlier as the Victoria Aristocrats.

In those days the east played the west, as in the CFL: the Montreal Canadiens, led by such future legends as Aurel Joliat and Georges Vezina, invaded the west to play against a band of Cougars owned, managed, coached, and centred by Lester Patrick.

The games were held at the 3,500-seat Willows Arena at Fort and Epworth in Oak Bay, a suburb of Victoria. Willows, built at a cost of $110,000, had opened with a gigantic skating party on a warm Christmas Day in 1911. The rink was closer to today's European standard, being a full 10 feet longer than the average NHL ice surface. But the important thing was that it was the first artificial ice rink in Canada. Over 800 Victorians made it a party to remember. Several thousand more were in the stands, gleefully watching the bodies pile up on the ice. In early January, the first professional hockey game west of Ontario was played there. Three days later, the Patrick family opened an arena in Vancouver. It was the largest artificial ice surface in the world.

The Cougars easily won the Stanley Cup in 1925. Their goalie was Bert Lindsay, father of former Red Wing great ''Terrible'' Ted Lindsay. The following year Victoria travelled to Montreal to play in the first Stanley Cup final held in the spanking-new Montreal Forum. They lost in a best-of-five showdown with the legendary Montreal Maroons.

The major innovations that led to the game as we know it originated at the Patrick family home on the corner of Linden and Chapman in Victoria. It had been traditional for defence-men to position themselves in front of each other, a set-up adapted from the point and counter-point positions in lacrosse. The Patrick brothers changed that. In addition, the introduction of the blue lines, forward passing at centre ice, the legal kicking of the puck, the numbering of the players to promote printed programme sales, the greater flexibility of the goaltender in being able to flop to his knees, changing players on the fly, the playoff series, the penalty shot, and the awarding of an assist following a goal were just some of the innovations that the Patrick brothers developed and introduced to the game. Eric Whitehead's *The Patricks: Hockey's Royal Family*, gives the whole fascinating story. Victoria never got another chance at the Stanley Cup, but its great hockey tradition is revived each time the junior Cougars take the ice in the aptly-named Memorial Arena in downtown Victoria.

Vancouver also has a hockey history that, blessedly, goes beyond the current Canucks.

In 1915 the Vancouver Millionaires defeated the Ottawa Senators in three straight games to win the Stanley Cup. The team was assembled by Frank Patrick, who simply raided the NHA (National Hockey Association) in the east and bought approximately two dozen of their best players. Frank and brother Lester founded the PCHA or Pacific Coast Hockey Association in the fall of 1911. The Vancouver club competed with the Victoria Aristocrats and a team from New Westminster named the Royals. The PCHA was financed by the sale of the Patrick Lumber Company sawmill in Crescent Valley, 20 miles southwest of Nelson, BC. The Millionaires played their games in the Patrick Arena situated at the corner of Denman and Georgia, at the entrance to Stanley Park. Its seating capacity of nearly 11,000 made it second only to New York's Madison Square Garden in size on the North American continent. And the Millionaires had won the Stanley Cup a full decade before their arch-rivals in Victoria.

By 1925 hockey on the west coast was a losing proposition. Seattle was the first to fold and, with two teams left, the Pacific Coast Hockey Association became history. A Western Canada Hockey League was formed, but this was merely the last gasp.

The Eastern NHL was solidifying and expanding into the United States in Boston, Pittsburgh, and New York. These new teams were in the market for bona fide players. They had money to spend. The Patricks sold players to the NHL in bunches. Lester became coach of the New York Rangers; sons Muzz and Lynn soon followed their father. To use Tiger Williams' phrase, the West Coast was "done like dinner."

War On Ice

You live by the sword, you die by the sword.
— Old Testament NHL proverb
I went to the fights and a hockey game broke out.
— Rodney Dangerfield

It is Sunday in Piestnay, Czechoslovakia. The Canadian junior team is playing the Soviets in the final game of the 1987 international junior championships. The Canadians are dominating the Soviets, leading 4-2 midway through the second period and threatening to add to their total. Our chance for the gold is on the line. We need to win by four to secure the medal. The Russians, already out of gold medal contention, resort to stickwork in an attempt to provoke the Canadians. The usual endless shoving and scuffling after the whistle develops near the Canadian goal. Suddenly, two players drop their gloves and go at it. This is a ''no-no'' in international hockey; the prescribed penalty is automatic ejection from the game. The Russian bench erupts, the players pouring over the boards to aid their stricken comrade. Outmanned and clearly outgunned, the Canadian bench feels compelled to follow. A

131

full-scale brawl breaks out, resulting in the eventual disqualification of both teams. The Soviets, last in the tournament and having nothing to lose, forfeit a game they've already lost. The Canadians lose their chance to win the tournament the instant they come off the bench. This brawl is the Canadians' second of the tournament. Their earlier match against the Americans opened with a pre-game punch-up. The final fiasco brings international shame and disgrace on both our team and our country.

Back home, 94 per cent of Canadians watching the game on TV approve of the action taken by their team. They know that no NHL team would look at a player who did not come to the assistance of his teammates. It is the law of the jungle; it is the code of the game.

Under the circumstances, what choice did they have? As a former coach, my initial reaction would have been to hold my players for 30 seconds or so — to make clear to everyone who was first over the boards — and then urge my guys to go get 'em. But this approach would not have altered the outcome. Don Cherry's reaction was to go get 'em right away, and reaction is a key word in hockey. As Cherry said on reflection: "You don't really think in hockey, you react all the time."

A successful winning attitude calls for a depth of discipline rare among 18-year-olds faced with a frightened and incompetent international referee who's lost control of the game. But a coach has a great deal of time before the game, and some time between each period, to think of all possible responses, and to have his players react to deliberate intimidation by filling the opposition net rather than the penalty box. One has the choice of taking the frustration and turning it into additional energy to play a strong game and score lots of goals, or to turn it into anger, chippiness, and cheap shots.

Though he later disavowed his statement, it was Conn Smythe, former manager of the Toronto Maple Leafs, who first said: "If you can't beat 'em in the alley, you can't beat 'em on the ice," but this expression is fundamentally Canadian in that it springs from our whole northern frontier pioneer-settlement experience. Our rough and rowdy Crazy Canuck ways are freely acknowledged everywhere but at home.

The Canadian performance at Vimy Ridge was a mixture of raw courage and bravado. Pierre Berton states that a whole generation of outgoing, exuberant, risk-taking Canadians was lost to us in that famous battle. Their shadows remain only on the downhill slopes and on the ice.

In an article in *Holiday* magazine, Hugh MacLennan once described hockey as "the counterpart of the Canadian self-restraint. To spectator and player alike, hockey gives the release that strong liquor gives a repressed man." For some rabid fans — and equally rabid players — hockey is our national tonic. It is nothing to be ashamed of.

The popular image of the hockey player is a macho, blood and guts, rough, tough, barrel-chested, beer-drinking man like Dave Schultz, former Oiler Dave Semenko, Calgary's Tim Hunter, Joey Kocur of Detroit, or Dave Brown of the Flyers. These are considered virile young men, combining fitness and enthusiasm with a dose of Canadian humility — off the ice. The camaraderie that comes from rough play is their real reward. For these men there are no trophies, least of all the NHL award for the most gentlemanly player. It is called the "Lady" Byng. Who of the above would want to win it?

"We practised violence because we knew it won hockey games. The other teams were afraid of us. Which meant we had the puck most of the time." So spoke Derek Sanderson, a machismo glamour boy of the mid-70s big bad Bruins, a team that combined the glorious talents of Bobby Orr and Phil Esposito with the street tactics of a Sanderson or Wayne Cashman. Fred Shero, the Philadelphia Flyer coach who built an NHL championship team based on such tactics once said: ''To beat Boston, you do the same thing to Orr that Clarke did to Kharlamov. Break his ankle.'' His captain, Bobby Clarke, was one of the meanest players to ever play the game.

In his best-selling book *Tiger*, former Leaf and Vancouver Canuck Dave Williams contends that professional hockey players consent ''to some form of assault'' when they skate out onto the ice. Williams says that there is ''a part of you that is completely shut off'' from reality when you're playing the game.

Fan violence is not a concern in the NHL, at least not yet, though St Patrick's night 1955 will be remembered by hockey fans all over North America as the night of the Richard riot.

The Rocket had tangled with Hal Laycoe of the Bruins a week before the season ended. During their tussle, Richard had inadvertently struck a linesman. He was suspended for the remainder of the season by league president Clarence Campbell, thereby losing his only chance to win the league scoring title, the closest he ever came.

A tear gas bomb exploded at the Canadiens next home game, forfeited to Detroit. Angry fans poured out onto St Catherine St, joining with others who had been waiting for something to happen. Shop windows were smashed, looting occurred, bonfires were set in the street. Damage was estimated at over $100,000.

It is often said that the subsequent rise of Quebec nationalism that was to result in a separatist victory two decades later had its genesis in the Richard riot of March 17, 1955.

Those who feel that the game is too violent today have little sense of hockey history. During the 1904 Ontario Hockey Association season, there were four on-ice deaths.

Frank Patrick of the famous Patrick family once spoke of a game he refereed between Cornwall, Ontario and a team from Montreal. One of the Cornwall players opened ''a Montreal player's skull with his stick'' and Patrick, having assigned the Cornwall player a penalty that determined the outcome of the game, barely escaped with his life. The following weekend, another Cornwall player was killed by being clubbed over the head. Later in his career, Frank Patrick and the legendary Newsy Lalonde clubbed each other unconscious with well-aimed sticks to the skull.

Frank's brother Lester told of being cut over the eye for 12 stitches, while a teammate was run over by a skate and had to leave the game with a badly gashed foot. Several other players received broken noses and cuts about the eyes. All of this took place in the same game.

Hod Stuart was probably the game's first policeman. Lester Patrick felt he owed his life to Stuart for coming to his rescue in a 1907 battle between the Ottawa Senators and Patrick's Montreal Wanderers. Next day the Montreal papers used such phrases as ''a saturnalia of blood-letting'' and ''the most sordid exhibition of butchery ever seen in hockey,'' ''an exercise in primitive savagery,'' and ''quite literally, a bloody disgrace.'' This was in 1907.

In those early days it was said that players fought simply to keep warm. However, the late Frank ''King'' Clancy, one of hockey's legendary figures, wrote: ''I guess we were sadists. A lot of hockey players are.'' Clancy had a role in the Bailey-Eddie Shore fracas of December 12, 1933, the game where Bailey was nearly killed.

The Leafs and Bruins were engaged in a hard-fought contest. Eddie Shore, the Ty Cobb of hockey, was tripped up by Clancy or possibly Red Horner. Shore went after Bailey, mistaking him for one of the Toronto defencemen, and pole-axed him from behind. Horner, outraged at Shore's unnecessary attack on Bailey, punched Shore to the ice. Shore's head hit with terrific force, splitting open.

Ace Bailey survived two brain operations, but his playing days were over. Eddie Shore returned to the Boston team, wearing a helmet.

Previously in his career Shore had suffered ''a lacerated cheekbone, a two-inch cut over his left eye, a broken nose, three broken teeth, and two black eyes,'' all in one game. As well, he'd once been knocked out for over 10 minutes. In his quarter century in the big leagues, Eddie Shore absorbed almost a thousand stitches.

When I was a young fan in Montreal, Detroit's ''Old Scarface,'' ''Terrible'' Ted Lindsay was the original Mr Tough-Guy, though he had considerable opposition from the likes of little Tony Leswick, Fernie Flaman, Leo Labine, and the aptly-named Wild Bill Ezinicki. Lindsay, whose face was as craggy as WH Auden's, was rumoured to have been the first to have said: ''The hockey stick is the great equalizer.'' Lindsay's swordwork in jousts with Ezinicki were the talk of hockey in the '50s. The ''other'' Howe, brother Vic, played for Detroit against the hated Leafs of that era, then led by Turk Broda, Jimmy Thomson, *et al*. In a newspaper interview Howe commented: ''They were fighting all the time.''

Later that same decade, ''Leapin' Louie'' Lou Fontinato inherited the title of Mr Tough-Guy in the NHL. One evening the Rangers' Eddie Shack collided with Gordie Howe behind the net. They exchanged punches. Fontinato saw a golden opportunity to solidify his reputation as NHL heavyweight champion and raced to Shack's defence. Howe, an incredibly strong man and one of the finest players ever to play the game, took Fontinato's initial flurry of blows without flinching. Then, he turned on Fontinato and delivered a series of blows that broke Fontinato's nose and reduced his face to pulp. It was said that Howe had planted his skates against the back of the net to get greater leverage and more wallop in his punch. Whatever the case, Howe went on to further greatness, practising his skills within an ever-widening circle of respect whenever he was on the ice. Few players dared to check Howe closely. Lou Fontinato's heavyweight career — and hockey career — were over.

One of the strangest episodes I remember occurred in an exhibition game in 1969, two years after expansion, and about the time I began to lose interest in the game. One of the least exciting expansion teams, the St Louis Blues, were playing the Bruins in Ottawa. Ted Green, Boston's big policeman, was checked by Wayne Maki behind the Bruin cage. In a meaningless pre-season game, Green shoved Maki to the ice, Maki retaliated, Green retaliated, striking Maki on the shoulder with his stick, and Maki whacked Green over the head with the bend of his stick — its strongest part — nearly killing Green. He required a two-and-a-half hour operation to put a steel plate in his head. Ironically, Maki was found to be suffering from a brain tumour and died five years later.

Every fan of the game can make up his or her own list of fights but one thing is certain: hockey is a rough, tough, high-risk game of instantaneous action and reaction. One can get hurt playing it, just as one can get hurt crossing the street. But there are differences. There has always been one law on the ice and another away from the rink.

Former coach Scotty Bowman once hired Jean-Guy Talbot
to be his assistant coach. Most fans recalled it was Talbot who
struck Bowman in the eye, ending the latter's NHL career.
Those who've played the game would not be surprised at
Bowman's decision. As Hugh Hood explains, in his book on
Jean Beliveau: "The situation down on the ice in the middle
of play is an *abstract* situation, a sort of code for life, not just
the same as life, and certain ordinary rules are temporarily
suspended."

When did the policeman, equalizer, enforcer, hit man, and
peacemaker (surely a misnomer) become a goon? When did the
"normal" fisticuffs become gratuitous, the policeman transformed first to intimidator and, then, finally, terminator?

Many current fans feel that goon hockey was born with
Dave Schultz. In the spring of 1973 the Philadelphia Flyers
won the Stanley Cup, and led the league in penalties, the first
time a team had accomplished both feats. By the mid-'70s,
winning was synonymous with intimidation. Coach Fred Shero
told his players that the key to winning hockey games was
"to arrive at the net with the puck and an ill humour." Flyer
captain Bobby Clarke, now general manager of the team,
summed up this mentality when he asked: "If you swear at
me, who's the instigator of the fight if I hit you?" The Wings'
Joey Kocur, asked if he was worried about rough stuff in the
'87 Toronto-Detroit quarter-final playoff, claimed he wasn't
worried, adding: "We've got enough stupids here."

In his book, *The Hammer: Confessions of a Hockey
Enforcer*, Schultz describes how he used fighting as a tactic to
get his team going. "Fighting can lead to momentum," he
wrote. He sums up his own attitude toward the game in this
odd comment from *The Hammer*: "...there was only one
way for me to overcome my Mennonite background and that

was to go completely wild in the other direction.'' However wild Schultz became, hockey is one of the few channels where his Dr Jekyll-Mr Hyde transformation would not only be allowed, but encouraged. Dan Maloney, coach of the Winnipeg Jets, said recently: ''In hockey, it's not how many fights you win. It's how many you show up for.''

There is a considerable lack of spontaneity when goon battles goon but at least it is within the limits of the unwritten hockey code. Most goon fighting is premeditated; it is understood that it is an exhibition staged mainly for the assembled throng and the millions watching on TV. Goon against goon does not violate the gentleman's agreement that occasional fights always stay within certain limits.

Like war, hockey has always had its code of conduct. Goons are to brawl only with goons, fighters are to fight only their own, superstars are to be left alone, goaltenders are off-limits.

Schultz confesses he was often jealous when playing against the likes of Bryan Trottier, Marcel Dionne, or Guy Lafleur, but that he had no ''sense of vindictiveness'' when on the ice with such superstars. In fact, Schultz had ''a great appreciation of their talents.'' He was bound by the code.

The code is dictated and agreed upon by the players. They are the ones who determine its limits, set its parameters. When one of these unwritten rules is broken, trouble lies ahead. And when violations occur, it is the players who must deal with the violator, not the referee. The latter merely arbitrates the degree of violent response, he does not determine it. If the prevailing code of conduct is upheld, the players settle their ritual differences and return to the proper business of playing the game the way it was meant to be played. Frequently, opposing players who have fought on ice are friends once away from the arena. In last spring's quarter-final playoffs, Toronto's Rick Vaive and the Blues Rob Ramage bumped and bruised each other at every opportunity throughout the six-game series. Vaive and Ramage were the best of friends, and had once been roommates early in their careers.

There is no question that our society has a deep admiration for "fighters" and that this admiration is transposed to the ice. Even as we think how wrong it is we feel how good it feels. In a playoff game in 1984, Dale Hunter of the Nordiques squared off against his brother, Mark, who then played for the Canadiens. Their father, who was in the stands, adopted a typically Canadian approach. He pulled for whoever seemed to be losing.

The media hype that promotes team against team, good guys against bad guys, Edmonton against Philadelphia, could be greatly defused if players made more sportsmanlike gestures toward each other during the course of a game. This would serve to keep the participant and the fan cognizant of the fact that a game rather than a war is being played out. Some team owners are as much to blame as the media.

One-time back-up junior A goalie Greg Richardson remembers how veteran players pressured the younger ones to fight. Richardson recalls current Canuck Barry Pederson going around the dressing room congratulating those players who'd fought in a brawl in the previous period. Richardson says: "It left the others embarrassed, with the feeling that they didn't do their part." During the season, veterans constantly reminded younger players — and some older ones — that to stay on the team they'd better fight when challenged. Richardson says that if, after a while, a player was still not fighting, a veteran would start a fight with the younger player in practise.

He remembers Torrie Robertson, now of the Hartford Whalers, and Paul Cyr, currently with Buffalo, doing this on several occasions when both were members of the Victoria Cougars. However, Richardson was quick to point out that the smaller players — and any exceptional player — were excluded from all this roughness.

Even in training camp in Penticton, Richardson says the coach would send a veteran player or two out to challenge and fight young prospects to find out if the young novices could take it. Richardson was excused from such tactics because he was a goalie but he got the distinct impression that to make junior A hockey you had to fight. There is little or no fighting in senior hockey leagues because the players are considered too old for the NHL. As a consequence, there are no NHL scouts sitting in the sparsely filled stands to be impressed by toughness.

''When I see what's happening in hockey,'' says Serge Savard, ''tough kids jumping on other players' backs to pound them — I doubt I want my son participating in such a game.''

In a *Playboy* article, the interviewer suggested to Wayne Gretzky that hockey ''still seems more violent than other sports,'' and Gretzky said that's ''because there is fighting. In other sports, I believe, if you fight, you're automatically ejected from the game. In hockey, you're not, the reason being that you're carrying around a hockey stick, a lethal weapon.'' The implication here is that fighting is not nearly as dangerous as whatever you can do with your stick. Gretzky goes on to say that he'd be ''more scared standing in front of the plate with the pitcher throwing a ball 100 mph at my head.'' He concludes: ''Nobody's ever been really hurt in hockey fights.'' Certainly, it is not easy to throw punches while trying to maintain one's balance on quarter-inch skate blades. Not to mention the lack of leverage. Later in the interview, Gretzky concurs with those old-time fans and former players who feel that the game was a great deal rougher in the 1960s.

Rougher it certainly was, but, almost without exception, the rough and tough players also had high-calibre hockey skills. John Ferguson often potted 20 goals. Ted Lindsay was one of the best players in the game. There were no goons, and no policemen who only "policed." The birth of the goon occurred about the time of expansion, when players who would never have made the NHL were suddenly in the league. As well, there was a great need to sell the game to American audiences, who, by and large, knew little or nothing about hockey but a great deal about wrestling, boxing, and roller derby. *Sports Illustrated* editorialized with apparent glee that a new reporter, assigned to cover the NHL, had a brother who "...achieved a measure of fame in the Philadelphia area when TV cameras at a Flyers game caught him leaning over the ice to menace an official, and a local cable company used the clip in promo spots the next season." *SI* also felt it worthy to add to their reporter's qualifications that his younger brother Mark hucked spitballs "onto the helmets of several Calgary Flames as they sat on the bench. 'They stayed on through an entire shift,' says Mark proudly." Rumour has it that when Gordie Howe was playing for Houston, he was approached by a glamourous southern belle as he was leaning on the boards. "What is that itty-bitty 'lil thang down there?" she asked. It was the puck. The story might be hearsay, but it was true that the NHL could hardly bank on American viewers knowing the game.

Canadian novelist Jack Ludwig, in New Orleans for Mardi Gras in 1973, commented: "I watched an NHL commercial on a local news broadcast. New Orleans, as a city marked for NHL expansion, was being fed the Sunday games, getting

warmed up for bayou skaters. The NHL commercial empha-
sized brawling, and pure show biz — not as crude as late-night-
show wrestling, not as hokey as roller-derby pile-ups, but just
as exciting as a motorcyclist busting up on parked buses.''

Such an emphasis on show biz and brawling has taken an
international flavour. Ads for hockey fights on video are now
common in hockey magazines, and for only 99 cents at the
local video store any kid can rent *Hockey Fights Vol. 1* or
Hockey Fights Vol. 2. Cliff Fletcher, general manager of the
Calgary Flames, sees nothing wrong with marketing professional hockey as pure entertainment. Fighting sells tickets.
Conn Smythe felt the same way. ''We've got to stamp out
that kind of thing,'' he was once quoted as saying, ''or people
are going to keep on buying tickets.''

The reason why referees seldom if ever call penalties in
the playoffs — and never in the last several minutes or overtime of a game — has seldom been examined. The reason most
often given is that the league does not wish the referees to
influence the outcome of a game. This is true as far as it goes,
but it doesn't go far enough.

NHL referees do not decide how to call games, the league
decides. Al Strachan has written that, by not calling the stickwork, interference, and holding that were dominant in the
Stanley Cup playoffs in the early rounds, ''the league is
saying that it feels action, flow, speed and grace are not to be
rewarded. It is saying that fans would prefer to see stick-
grabbing, interference, holding and late hits.''

Many fans, however, are offended by the goonery, brawls,
and bench-clearing skirmishes — the pulling, the shoving, the
pairing-off, and the seemingly endless milling about that so
dilutes the game and destroys its natural rhythm. Yet, in our
society violence means money. Today's box office hits and

bestsellers are evidence enough. The NHL caters to a lowest common denominator when it allows goons to destroy the very game it is trying to promote.

The *Globe and Mail* once ran a picture of Gordie Howe at a hockey school in Peterborough, Ontario. He has one knee on the ice, obviously in a relaxed mood, giving tips to the youngsters present and posing for photographers. Behind him, the reason for the photo, Howe's grinning grandson, age eight, is cross-checking his famous grandfather across the back of the neck. The caption reads: "Howe To Do It."

Young boys search for a sense of excitement. Hockey is fast-paced, rough and tough, a challenge; in short it has all the ingredients that a young teenager misses from his earlier years. Hockey tends to bring out the man in the boy, or else.

From the outset I was a poor skater, because I started late, but I knew all the moves — even if I didn't have them — and I loved hitting. Away from the rink I still stuttered and was shy, but on ice my body did the talking. And I had a knack for scoring goals, having watched others turn the trick against me when I was in the nets. Though I was not conscious of it then, hockey was giving me the confidence to assert myself off ice; to become part of the real, male world.

Players in the NHL, playing on a smaller ice surface than European players, are often chosen for their toughness as much as for their ability.

It cannot be said often enough that hockey is played on ice, at speeds up to 30 mph, in a confined, restricted space — all of which makes hockey a potentially dangerous game. Risk is ever-present.

Claudia Thompson, mother of a seven-year-old hockey player told me: "I felt guilty dressing him for this, if something should happen. I didn't want to see him hurt.'' In October 1982 young Normand Leveille, a promising Bruin winger, was hit by a solid bodycheck in a game in Vancouver and slid into the boards. He suffered a cerebral hemorrhage. It was doubtful he'd live. Today, he can walk, say a few words, sit up, eat, drive a specially-designed car, answer the phone. His passion is still hockey. The most he can hope for is a position as a minor-league instructor in the Boston organization. Leveille was a victim of an accident in a high-speed, high-risk game. Violence was not a factor.

The difference between playing rough and playing dirty is an abstract one, impossible to define. Jim Dorey, former defenceman for the Leafs, came as close as anybody: ''A tough guy will slam you into the boards every time he can, and if he fights, it's just a natural reaction from the heat of the game. But a mean player, he'll try and hurt you. He'll use his stick. He'll plot to get you when nobody's looking.''

Pierre Pilote, one of the all-time great Blackhawk defencemen, was asked by a reporter to talk about Gretzky. Pilote replied: ''Years ago, Gretzky wouldn't have been able to freewheel like he does. Somebody would have speared him; they would have had to carry him off the ice.''

Amazingly enough, Wayne Gretzky himself feels that he would have been hard pressed to play then, too. In his *Playboy* interview Gretzky said: ''I might never have played 20 years ago. I remember people saying to me 10 years ago that I might not make it, because I was too small. No, 20 years ago, I definitely would not have been able to play in the NHL.''

Gretzky's explanation of why he doesn't get hit so often is equally interesting. He attributes this to the fact that he — like many NHLers — played lacrosse. In the same interview he explained: ''In lacrosse, there's always cross-checking. You learn to roll with the checks and never get hit straight on ... I learned when I was a kid that it's tougher to hit a moving target than a target that's standing still.''

Most players love the bodychecking aspect of the game. A good body checker feels like a cat prowling for food. Claire Johnson of Montreal says: ''My oldest boy is 5'6'' and weighs 145 lbs. He loves to check and once told me joyously, 'Hey, Mom, the guy put me in the air up over the boards.' ''

I learned early how to hug the boards. I was shown how a player can decrease the space between himself and the boards to allow little room between you and those unyielding, unforgiving planks. I realized at the time that this was the physics of hockey; you take the concussive check, its full force, and you ride or flow with it. You become one with the force, because every inch of the check magnifies the check approximately 10 times.

Nevertheless, checks from behind — however legal — can be dangerous, as in the case of the case of the career-ending spinal injury to Brad Hornung of the Regina Pats; that is why we were taught never to let them happen to us. From the time I began playing, I had it drilled into me that you never, ever put your head down when you're on the ice. This was especially true if you were anywhere near the boards. Yet, constantly, even when watching junior A hockey, I see wingers crossing the opposition blueline, staring down at the puck on their sticks, as if amazed how it ever got there. Checks from behind are dangerous, but still, at this writing, legal. But the so-called ''finishing'' check, so popular nowadays — where the checker stays with the opposing player — is interference, and should be called.

Many past and present players I spoke to said that hockey appears much more ''violent'' to the spectators than it really is. Players are used to the roughness and toughness of the game. One veteran told me he'd noticed that his tolerance for pain had increased over the years. It is certainly true that players think nothing of a few stitches, large bruises, or a separated shoulder. They come to accept pain as part of their job, part of their life. Who can forget Bobby Baun finishing a Stanley Cup final game on a broken ankle. For most of them, an injury is not painful but an inconvenience.

"I see what other people see, but I also think a coach has a chance to see a little deeper, right into the soul of the game. And what I see as the soul of a hockey game is a tough man who never backs up." So spake Punch Imlach in his book *Hockey is a Battle*. And being tough and playing rough means the survival of the fittest. Those who are weak-kneed or injured had better look out. In *The Game of Our Lives* Peter Gzowski overheard Glen Sather discussing the Calgary Flames in the Edmonton dressing room. Sather is quoted as saying: "Dougie Riseborough has been the key to his team recently.... He's a gutsy player who doesn't make any headlines, but if you can slow him down you can slow a lot of them down. I don't want to say too much, but he's got a bad shoulder." When word came that Kharlamov might return for the final minutes of game seven of the '72 series, Jack Ludwig reported that coach Harry Sinden said to his players: "I don't want any of you guys to go out of your way, but if he (Kharlamov) happens to skate by, and gets in your way, give him a tickle." This is akin to stalking prey.

The toughest NHLers I saw play were often some of the smallest players in the league: "Terrible" Ted Lindsay, Fernie Flaman, Tony Leswick, who was 5'6" and weighed 160 lbs, Boston's Wayne Cashman, and that mightiest of mites, Leo Labine, who, when discussing his skill with the stick, coined the immortal Canadian phrase: "I don't know anyone who likes to eat wood, unless he's a beaver."

The late Lloyd Percival, Canada's internationally famous physical fitness expert, once wrote: "In a game like hockey you have to have the emotional ability to keep going despite the knocks, without overreacting to the dangers." In the end the game may teach self-assertion more than any other quality. Superstars such as Richard, Howe, and Orr had to continually assert themselves in order to establish a territorial circle within which no opponent would dare enter. Those great players who did not establish such an untouchable space, such as Bobby Hull, left the game before their time. There is little doubt that the time Orr spent establishing his physical presence shortened his career. When challenged, he fought. Yet not to have done so would have been worse. Like Doug Riseborough's shoulder mentioned earlier, Orr's knee injuries were making him increasingly vulnerable to the cheap shots of expansion-type players who had neither the talent nor the skills to play the game well. Over the years, Orr became a slower and slower target for such unsavoury tactics. As he once said: "I didn't want to fight, but if they see you backing up in this league, it's no good."

When I played organized hockey in the '50s, a young player would never think of bringing his stick up above his shoulders. When, for one reason or another, it did happen, someone would always skate by and tell the player to keep his stick down. Or you would feel a hand on your stick — not grabbing and holding it, or tucking it under the armpit as players do now — but simply pushing it down, down to ice level.

It's no coincidence that the increase of gratuitous violence in the game has occurred at the same time as an increase in the equipment worn by players. One minor-leaguer I spoke to felt that the increased protection gave players "a license to kill" and to use their stick with what he termed "tomahawk strokes."

The enhanced equipment increases the requirement for contact. Bobby Hull feels that current NHLers are wearing too much equipment. Recently Hull told a reporter: "I couldn't play in crap like that. Now that players are wearing helmets and visors, sticks are around the eyes all the time because they think they can't hurt anyone."

There are more eye injuries now than ever before because sticks are carried higher, and players feel it doesn't matter because everyone is protected. At the high speeds the game is currently played at, you have more balance but you carry your stick higher to maintain your balance. Holding the stick up more and more, the chances of getting clothes-lined or blindsided are much greater. Everyone talks of wearing faceshields — and many players do — but few suggest keeping the sticks down below the shoulder. I played hockey — organized and otherwise — for eight years without a helmet or visor, while wearing eye glasses, like Al Arbour. I was a digger. A checker. In eight years, I never got hurt playing the game.

I don't wish to be crass, but I recall a coach of mine — either Dick Irvin Jr or Cliff Fletcher — telling us that if we got hurt playing it was probably the result of a fluke, an accident, or the result of us not being knowledgeable about the game. The possibility of stupidity on someone else's part was seldom mentioned. We were taught to play the game like one is taught defensive driving. And it was simpler in those days, 30 years ago. Sporting solid tube skates, you could always hear someone coming. Now, skates are plastic or acrylic and both these materials serve to dampen sound. Helmets serve the same purpose. They diminish one's hearing and affect one's perception. These "Walkmans of the ice" insulate the contemporary hockey player and leave him more susceptible to injury. Recent Canadian Safety Association approved helmets were found to reduce peripheral vision by eight per cent and also reduce hearing.

Not long ago, in a neighbourhood bar, a stern advocate of wearing helmets said to me: "I think helmets are great. I suffered an eight-stitch cut on my forehead playing hockey, and it wouldn't have happened if I'd been wearing a helmet." "Well, what did happen?" I asked. "Oh, I got checked," he said, "a perfectly good check, and I fell and bumped my forehead on the ice." "Were you hurt?" I asked. "Oh, no," he said, "not at all, but it wouldn't have happened if I'd been wearing a helmet."

Earl Seibert, a defenceman in the '20s and '30s with the Hawks, Rangers, and Red Wings, was the first player to wear a helmet, after suffering a concussion. Seibert was once accused of dealing a death blow to Howie Morenz. It was Seibert who decked Morenz, sending the speedy star into the boards and breaking his leg in four places. Morenz died shortly afterward, but it is rumoured that it was his many well-wishers, who plied him with drinks while he was in hospital, who actually did the job.

When Minnesota's Bill Masterton died following a fall in a game in 1968, more players began to experiment with wearing a helmet, though Masterton's death was clearly an accident, similar to the thousands of accidents that happen every year on the highways, on the tracks, and in the air all across the nation.

Boston general manager Harry Sinden had some interesting comments to make to a reporter after veteran left winger

Charlie Simmer suffered an eye injury that, while not serious, kept him out of the game for several weeks. ''The kid didn't mean to hit him in the eye,'' Sinden told a Boston reporter, ''but he's been helmeted and visored all his career and he's got no respect for what can happen when you carry your stick up like that. Before this league had players running around looking like Knights of the Round Table, players had respect for injuries they could cause.''

> I was taught that the stick was for passing, taking a pass, shooting and scoring, but after watching... (the 1978) Stanley Cup series, we've turned it into an instrument of intimidation.
>
> — Jean Beliveau, in Hugh Hood's
> *Strength Down Centre*

Why is the stickwork permitted in today's game? Why the innumerable irritants or ''garbage'' that Bryan Trottier complained about publicly, ''the holding, the clutching, the grabbing'' and such interference that slows the game down and reduces the excitement for the fans and frustrates the players?

Interference is seldom called these days, nor is illegal motion. The rule regarding the face-off circle is a case in point. Now the players are never straight. Their skates must be on the two parallel red lines, either between them or on them at most. Now, players turn 30 degrees or more, but they should be straight as needles 'til the linesman's hand comes down. While this is going on, all the players that are at the circle are edging forward, into the circle, two, three, four feet. This is a creeping distortion of the game.

Such rule bending has been sullying the game since expansion greatly reduced the quality of play. I gave up watching junior hockey for several years in the mid-70s and early '80s when the game became an irritation rather than enjoyment. At one stage it seemed to be impossible for a defenceman to make a pass from the point without having a forward rub one of his gauntlets in the defenceman's face, *after* the pass had been made. Such behaviour inevitably led to stickwork and fighting later in the game.

In Stan Fischler's *Slashing!*, Glen Sather is quoted as saying: "My surefire method of enraging the other guy is to put my big leather glove in a superstar's face before 20,000 people. I'll mush the glove in his face for a few seconds, and he'll be real embarrassed." It's little wonder that talented European players have some difficulty in adjusting to what former Canuck general manager Harry Neale called "all the other things that go on over here."

As young boys growing up in Montreal, my friends and I felt the game had an honour and glory all its own. To play poorly, or to play deliberately outside the rules, was to bring dishonour to the game. It was not done. During the time I played, I recall only one incident that could have resulted in serious injury.

Our team was behind a couple of goals at the outset of the second period and it was clear we were ineffectual and listless in our play. As a good bodychecker, I decided to try and perk the team up by throwing my weight around. On each shift I checked my man every time he had the puck, handing out solid hits that were hard but clean and not following through or finishing. Slowly, our team began to come alive, and we had several flurries around the opposing net; the scoring chances were beginning to come. At the end of one such flurry, after

the whistle had gone, I was standing still near the net, about to move away and return to the bench. I should have known better than to be stationary on the ice. I never saw what hit me. My neck whipped back and the back of my head hit the ice. Fortunately, it was not a serious blow. I had a slight concussion but was otherwise okay. But the job had been done. I felt dizzy for the rest of the game and had to sit on the bench, unable to take my regular shift. It was only later I heard that one of the opposing players had snuck up behind me, slipped his stick between one of my skates and the blade, and given a yank. It was a most effective means of cooling my immediate fervour but I have never forgotten the moment or the player who did it.

If infractions such as this were called interference, and penalized from the outset, players would not continue to practise such illegal manoeuvers. But, as mentioned earlier, the players are the ones who determine the way the game is played, not the officials or the league, and the responsibility for such dubious practises falls squarely on their shoulders. The players are to blame.

Hockey is one of the best examples of our ability to channel and defuse aggressive behaviour.

Psychologist Edward Whitmont has written of the way in which human need reveals itself as ''...fear, hostility, and the urge to violence.'' He goes on to say that ''Our human problem lies in the fact that our basic instinctual urges...include both social and antisocial drives.''

The problem is what to do with our antisocial urges in a contemporary society that wishes to suppress and repress natural feelings and urges. As Whitmont points out, we repress ''desire, joy, and aggression,'' and, as a consequence, destructive behaviour breaks out in our society.

155

Whitmont feels that "there is no more violence... nowadays than in the past," but that current cultural morals see violence as "no longer compatible with our moral conscience."

Former Toronto Maple Leaf defenceman Jim Dorey once explained: "I'm an emotional guy and hockey gives me a release for my emotions. If I get stalled in an elevator or a traffic jam, it builds up until I want to hit someone. But that's not acceptable in today's society. So I wait until I get on the ice. (There), things happen so fast you can't keep anything inside."

Whitmont feels that "our whole being is pervaded by a love of violence for its own sake." Witness the proliferation of hockey fight videos. Aggression must be respected, it can't be repressed. Hockey and sports in general allow for a more human approach within socially accepted channels. Wendel Clark, one of the most complete players in the game today, expresses the archetype of the hero as warrior.

Hockey, one of the few games with boards as physical limits, has an increasing intensity that often generates instant, unthinking retaliation. In an arena of 20,000 screaming fans, it's a little like being a gladiator in the pit.

Jim Dorey makes the connection between the game and life. "If a guy reacts like a bastard on the ice," says Dorey, "it makes him bitter, and so he takes it out on anyone he can. He becomes even meaner." John Ferguson, policeman for the Montreal Canadiens on their great Stanley Cup teams and now general manager of the Winnipeg Jets, showed an unusual understanding of his role in the game when he said: "I was the villain who made the game interesting. Without me, they'd have nobody to hate."

Aristotle, the ancient hockey philosopher, knew about natural aggression. He called it catharsis. A release of tension

156

and a purging of violent emotion through the playing of the game. The hockey hero serves as a psychological release, a modern warrior like Rambo, who, according to film director George Cosmatos, ''can do the fighting and the dirty work for us while we eat the popcorn.'' Fighting is a necessary release not only for the players but also for the pent-up emotions of the crowd. Konrad Lorenz, one of the foremost experts on animal aggression, has written that catharsis can be achieved by the spectator as well as the player. Lorenz sees the cathartic experience as ''the most important function of sport.''

The randomness or creative disorder of a hockey game is one of its greatest attractions. Almost nothing is predictable, anything can happen. The game appeals to the more irrational side of our behaviour. The natural instincts of change, aggressiveness, high risk, and potential chaos are not suppressed but given natural outlet in the game. Its very unpredictability is what makes hockey such an adrenalin-building, fascinating sport. When it's played as well as it was in the Rendez-Vous '87 Series, or in the Canada-Soviet Canada Cup showdown, you can almost feel the game breathe.

The 80-Game Grind:
The Business of Hockey

We played hockey because we loved it. Anything we got paid was considered a bonus.

— Rocket Richard

You must understand. This is a business. The NHL is a business. There will never be a Canadian division because Canadian teams don't sell well in the United States. It would be bad for business.

— John Ziegler, NHL President

In the 1986-87 season, the Oilers played 112 games in a little over eight months: 80 regular season games, 11 exhibitions, and 21 playoff games culminating in the Stanley Cup. The final game took place on the last day of May. In that same season, the average NHL player's salary was $158,000.

Grueling seasons and grossly inflated salaries have, in the last decade, invoked a seriousness that is leaching hockey's lifeblood. The NHL has long forgotten that things are better if they're done for fun. As Ken Dryden noted: "Remarkable though it might seem, as recently as ten years ago it was

159

possible to watch a hockey game and never once think how much its players were paid.''

In spite of their fantastic salaries, I get the feeling that NHLers today are constantly holding something back in play, not giving their all, simply hoping to survive the 80-game grind alive, and in one piece.

The extended schedule has not only made it impossible for current NHL teams to play at peak performance — both physically and psychologically — but it has changed the kind of new players being inducted. NHL scouts and general managers are convinced they must draft big, tough players. The theory is that small players can't stay against the big guys over the course of the season. This kind of thinking prompted Montreal to draft Doug Wickenheiser instead of 167-pound Denis Savard, who subsequently set a Chicago record by scoring 75 points in his rookie year. (Johnny Gagnon, who played on a line with Morenz and Joliat and was known as ''The Black Cat of Chicoutimi,'' weighed in at 140 pounds.)

The National Hockey League grew from 6 teams to 12 in April 1967 and from 12 to 14 in 1970. By 1973 there were 21 teams in the NHL. Travel schedules became insane.

By the mid-'70s, hockey was no longer a celebration, no longer a contest, no longer a game. It was business. It was entertainment used to promote a product. Now, in the '80s, even the bitter rivalry between the Montreal Canadiens and the Quebec Nordiques is no longer about hockey. It's about beer. Molson's owns the Habs and Carling O'Keefe owns the Quebec squad. Beer sales follow the fortunes of the teams.

In 1987, the first round of the playoff series was increased to a best four-out-of-seven. Again, money was the motive. There was a game every night on TV; even the most die-hard fan was exhausted and skipping games by the second week. Only greed can explain why there are 16 teams in the playoffs.

Greed has become the NHL password. Interviewed on Madison Square Garden Network, John Ziegler was asked if fighting should be done away with in the NHL. His response? "It doesn't matter to me. What matters to me is providing a product that people enjoy and want to go see... because I am in the entertainment business, and the measure to me is, Are people going to pay money to see this entertainment? And they are saying yes to it .... So, if it ain't broke, don't fix it."

Another blow to the integrity of the NHL has been the 18-year-old draft. The underage draft began in 1980, and junior hockey still hasn't recovered. Many teams lost their best players to the NHL since the eligibility age was lowered from 20 to 18. More importantly, the maturing process of young players has been short-circuited. As a result, many young players are rushed, and fail to become bona fide NHLers. Careers are sometimes destroyed before they've had a chance to begin. An extra year or so with a good junior team can provide leadership qualities and immeasurable confidence for a young player. Most 18- and 19-year-olds are simply not mature enough to take the pressure of playing in the NHL, both on and off the ice. NHL Players Association president Alan Eagleson has gone on record as saying that "as many as 50 players taken in the underage draft may have had their careers destroyed prematurely." In *Lions of Winter*, Guy Lafleur called the 18-year-old draft "a veritable disaster."

Ever since hockey was first televised in the mid-1950's, NHL games have seldom been anything but "great." The hype is essential. Television plus sports equals big business,

161

and sponsors will not buy air time if the game isn't "great."
American football has suffered the same influence. Hence the
extraordinary hoopla over the Super Bowl, a championship
game that is an "event" rather than the often banal affair it
really is. In *Nice Guys Finish Last*, Paul Gardner writes of
football sponsors today who employ a television director —
someone who can prolong pauses or interrupt the game to
call time-outs to suit commercial requirements. Gardner
recounts how, in one Super Bowl, the second-half kick-off was
taken twice because a commercial had been showing when the
first kick was made. All of this is done to produce "a better
game" for the viewing audience.

In hockey, too, so many concessions have been made
to the mass media that any observer of the game would have
long ago lost count. In a *Globe and Mail* interview, Lorne
"Gump" Worsley told Murray Malkin that "the only reason
(teams) went to two goalies was to speed up the game for
television."

TV does not follow the game well, only the puck. The
camera lens attempts to take the place of language, but it is
neither as subtle nor as articulate. "Image" becomes more
valued than skillful play; it is the bizarre action that draws the
eye, not the graceful, accurate one. The Tiger Williamses reign
supreme. All the goonery and exaggerated behaviours are
meant not for the fans at the game but for all us couch potatoes
nestled in front of our 45-inch projection screens at home. As a
result, the NHL seems more and more to resemble pro
wrestling in its hype of fighting and mayhem. To paraphrase
Harold Innis, our hockey players "are reduced to the status
of sandwich men."

When, on occasion, we become concerned about maintaining our cultural autonomy as Canadians, hockey is constantly neglected. Yet no game is so closely related to the cultural integrity of the country. No other game has been such a force in bringing our country together. We subsidize our railways, airlines, pipelines, and oil companies. When driven to the edge, we reluctantly support our broadcasting system, theatres, book publishing industry, and magazines. But what party in power would consider allowing tax incentives to community shareholders to support professional hockey in places like Saskatoon, Ottawa, Halifax, or Victoria? Much simpler to sell our game to the Americans, who will market it as a brawling circus side-show in such ''traditional'' hockey towns as Houston, Atlanta, and Los Angeles.

When the NHL shifted its head office from Montreal to New York — and elected an American as president of the league — it turned its back on Canada.

Selling into (or is it ''out to'') the American market has not been easy. The Americans had a lot to learn. In the 1984 *Playboy* interview with Gretzky, American freelance writer Scott Cohen and *Playboy* editors included such introductory remarks as: ''When a hockey player scores, which isn't often (hockey scores read like baseball scores), the last player to touch the puck gets credit for the goal.'' And *Time* magazine, shortly after, ran a photo of Gretzky evading a check with the caption: ''Everyone is braced for a shot when he is loose in his own end.'' Ah, yes, there's nothing quite like those 150-foot shots to scare the mask right off the goalie at the other end of the rink.

It has been difficult to sell the game south of the border for other reasons: Americans are often ignorant of what goes on outside their borders, ignorant of what goes on in the world.

163

They have great difficulty identifying with the Canadian teams, or even knowing where these teams come from. Hockey ranked 15th in sports popularity in a recent U.S. survey, behind roller derby and bowling. The fact that most European players (including the Soviets) see the NHL as the Holy Grail of hockey has little effect upon the insular Americans.

Pandering to this xenophobic attitude is not the answer, yet we are masterful at doing anything and everything to make the game amenable to U.S. sponsors. Saskatoon suffered from American myopia in 1983 and the same will likely happen to Hamilton when the NHL decides to further dilute its already thin talent. With expansion in 1967, the U.S. gained a great chunk of our national birthright. Since that time, an anti-Canadian bias has developed in the NHL.

In a nutshell, governors of American-based teams are not happy when Canadian teams come to town. The problem is that, unlike other major league sports, the National Hockey League does not share gate receipts. Many Canadian clubs are poor draws in the U.S. The Winnipeg Jets were the worst road draw of any club in the NHL in 1985- 86. Who can forget what Boston Bruins owner Art Mooney said during expansion talks in 1978: "What do we want a one horse cow town like Winnipeg in this league for?"

It's no secret that the National Hockey League is considering another expansion in 1989. The cities most frequently named are such natural territories as Dallas, San Francisco, Milwaukee, and possibly Seattle. Strangely enough, Halifax, Ottawa, Hamilton, and Saskatoon are rarely mentioned. These days, even the players are uneasy about playing in Canada because of our tax rules. The American tax structure attracts young rookies intent on making a million before they ever reach their stride in the NHL.

164

Selling the game to the Americans was our worst sin. Since expansion, the NHL has molded the game to suit the taste of American sponsors and viewers who are basically unfamiliar with hockey and who crave televised displays of crude aggression and machismo. It is no wonder that a complex, swift, and graceful game has sunk to a primeval lust for blood, that the traditions of the game are ignored or violated, that goonery, gratuitous violence, and unsportsmanlike behaviour are tolerated, even encouraged.

I don't believe that fans want to see the game reduced to its lowest common denominator, a kind of street hockey played by thugs — at least, I don't think that's what Canadian fans want. But the NHL demands parity among the teams; hence the draft and a whole slew of rules over the last decade that serve to make the game "more equal." The National Hockey League fears disparity because disparity means loss of ticket and TV revenue and loss of general interest — already so marginal — in American cities. I'm sure the league would have been much happier had Philadelphia won the Stanley Cup in '87 rather than the Oilers (have you noticed how the NHL front office frequently refers to American teams by city but Canadian teams by their nicknames?) for two reasons: First, the Oilers come from somewhere in Canada — Edmonton, isn't it? And secondly, the Oilers are in danger of becoming a dynasty, having won the Cup three times in the last four years. The NHL does not want dynasties, particularly Canadian ones. It costs them too much money.

And yet, some of what we get on the ice in Canada is still "the real thing." The greed of the National Hockey League has wounded but not yet destroyed our game.

Every contest has individual moments of grace and beauty:

165

an explosive rush, a perfect pass, an unbelievable save.

Hockey can be more than greed. Hockey can be the 1987 Canada Cup. Gretzky, Lemieux, Bourque, Fuhr, Gilmour. Canadian players transcending their own talents. At times like these, Canada exhibits the best ''product'' in the world.

The Puck Stops Here

Each goalie stands on a lonely island.

— Bernie Parent

If I missed one shot, (Coach) Tarasov would ask: 'What happened? Let us try and figure it out.'

— Vladislav Tretiak

It's a charity benefit game at the local hockey emporium in the middle of summer. The players are a mix of NHL stalwarts and junior A stars, with a few pickups and friends who have the ability to skate with the big boys. The pregame warmup session ends and the players store all the practise pucks in the back of each net. As the national anthem is played, both goalies — 180 feet apart and acting alone — slowly and methodically reach behind them with their sticks to fish out all the pucks. By the time the anthem and opening ceremonies are over, and the players break from their respective bluelines, each goaltender awaits the linesmen with a huge gloveful of pucks in his outstretched mitt.

Why does a young boy choose to go into the nets, when all his friends want to be forwards and score goals? What's the

167

big attraction? Why go between the pipes? Two reasons.

First, in the nets the goaltender meets his inexorable truth: that while it is fun to score goals, or, like a defenceman, have a hand in preventing them, his greatest satisfaction is stopping a ''labelled'' drive, making a spectacular save, recording a shutout.

Secondly, of all the players on the ice, the goaltender is often the intellectual, the introspective one, the odd man out. Tretiak and the Canadiens' former standout Ken Dryden are only two of the most recent examples. Tretiak is a serious reader and a lover of contemporary Russian literature, while Dryden, a lawyer, spent several months working with Ralph Nader's ''Raiders'' in Boston. These are thinking men, unusual in the game of hockey where most players rely on natural ability and reflexes.

You don't have to be neurotic to play nets but it probably helps. The psyche of the goaltender is determined at an early age. As a boy, he is often intuitive, reflective, passive, a loner. Goaltending is his way of quietly distinguishing himself with his peers — part of the team, one of the gang, but still an independent spirit, alone in the nets. At an age when being like everyone else is of utmost importance, he nevertheless finds himself compelled to go between the pipes, set apart from his teammates, intent on keeping things out. He gets an intense — almost nasty — pleasure from stopping the puck, an unconscious satisfaction in thwarting the aggressive male desire ''to score.''

When I was in nets there were times I felt like a gladiator, a medieval knight in hand-me-down armour, a hero, and there were times I felt like a sacrificial goat, a kind of Louis Riel on ice — all in the same game. There is something stirring, almost valiant, about the netminder standing, like Shakespeare's prince, ''naked and alone'' against the endless hordes of circling invaders sweeping into his territory and attacking his net.

For the goalie, there is a kind of masochistic attraction in knowing that, eventually, despite whatever he does, he will be beaten, momentarily defeated. It's only a matter of time before the red light flashes behind him signifying a personal failure. His sins are recorded for all to see in bright lights on the arena scoreclock high above the ice, and in the sports reports the next day. In addition, with instant replay, a goalie now looks bad again and again. All the natural forward aggression of the game is projected against him. After a losing effort, the other players agree, subconsciously, to label the goalie as the guilty one — and the goalie consents. The fans, less subtly, are quick to get on his back with chants of ''Sieve! Sieve!'' and applause when he stops a routine shot. His is a temporary but necessary sacrifice; he must bear the weight of the loss on his shoulders in order that his team may make a new beginning next game. He must do so willingly, aware of the differences between himself and his teammates that keep him in the nets, and in a web of his own making.

It is easy to see the goaltender as witness. There he stands, behind the scenes, out of the play for almost half the game. He looks on, attempting to keep himself mentally sharp and at the ready by rehearsing his last great save, or the one to come, over and over in his mind. Full of himself, he is, by turns, full of satisfaction *and* fear. The net is his sanctuary, a place where he can prove himself, a place where a quiet, reflective person-ality (off-ice) — like the Islanders' Billy Smith or the Flyers' Ron Hextall — can make a statement, both by stopping shots and by intimidating forwards. (Remember Hextall's vicious slash on Kent Nilsson in the '87 Stanley Cup final?)

On November 1, 1959, Jacques Plante went to the Canadiens' dressing room after being hit by a shot, and returned wearing a mask. Plante had a long history of playing with masks. A fine all-around athlete, he'd been a baseball catcher and a star goalie in lacrosse. He'd experimented with several masks, but only in practise, until that night Ranger great Andy Bathgate, parked directly in front of the crease, lifted a drive that almost tore Plante's nose from his face. When the injured netminder returned to the game sporting one of his practise masks, Coach Toe Blake was not amused. Blake felt that a goalie's reflexes would be affected because he'd relax a little and get too comfortable. But Plante was a great goaltender. When the Habs won 11 games in a row with the masked man in the cage — and won the Stanley Cup in 8 straight later the same year — Blake had nothing but praise for his masked marvel.

The masked goalie is here to stay, though Blake was not alone in his reservations. No less an authority than former Ranger and Canadien great Gump Worsley had some surprising comments to make about the mask in a *Globe and Mail* interview with Murray Malkin: ''I think things were safer for goalies in the days when they didn't wear a mask because in the beginning there was only the one-goalie system. Other players wouldn't poke around the net because they knew you were the only goalie and they respected you. They knew if you were injured, your team would get even and get their goalie back.'' Worsley's comments are interesting for two reasons: first, they suggest that the game was held in check by a players' code, or a series of unwritten rules, and secondly, that the more equipment one wears, the less the unwritten code applies. Though most NHL goalies deny it, they now get struck in the face more often than when they didn't wear a mask.

Clint Benedict, long-forgotten netminder for the Montreal Maroons in the 1920s, was the first to don a mask, after his nose and cheekbones were shattered by a drive off the stick of Howie Morenz. Made of leather, the mask was strapped on and covered his forehead, nose, cheeks, and chin. Abandoning it after a single game because it obscured his vision, Benedict's career was later ended by another Morenz shot, this time to the throat.

In recent years the fibreglass mask — specially molded to the face — has become a work of art. Ken Dryden's concentric C's were reminiscent of West Coast native Indian design, while Gilles Gratton of the Rangers sported a realistic cougar mask. Do contemporary netminders decorate their masks to ward off the evil intentions of the opposition? Are they designed to protect both the life *and* the soul of the goalie? Gerry Cheevers, former netminder of the Boston Bruins, used to wear a mask marked with all the scars he would have received in the line of fire had he not been wearing one.

Because of changes in the game over the years, the goalie has been forced not only to accept the mask, but to alter his entire style and approach. With the advent of the slapshot — and the curved stick that resembles a lacrosse racquet and whips the puck rather than shoots it, making it dip or drop unexpectedly — there are now places on the ice from which it is impossible for a netminder to react fast enough to have any chance of stopping the puck. Shots from close in now wing by like bullets — faster than a human being wearing 30 pounds of equipment can react, indeed, faster than human reflexes. As a result, the emphasis on goaltending is one of being in the right place at the right time, knowing how to play the angles, and having good lateral movement.

For as long as I can remember, we had a ping-pong table

in the basement of our house. My father, brother and I played for hours on end. Later, my high school friends came over after school and we'd hold round-robin tournaments that went on until they'd be called home for supper. I was so much better than my family and friends that I soon began playing two games at once: ping-pong on the "outside" and hockey in my head, concentrating with equal fervour on getting the point *and* blocking slams that whistled off the end of the table. I was particularly adroit at "kicking them out," using my legs and feet to knock the ping-pong ball down and keep it in front of me, though sometimes a quick left hand came into play, the same one that later became my glove hand in the nets. I'm convinced that the thousands of hours I spent playing ping-pong like this built the speed and cat-like reflexes which served me so well when I went between the pipes. Frozen tennis balls and flying pucks were easy after years of stopping a tiny, spinning, whizzing, dropping, curving ping-pong ball. When my ping-pong days were over, I took up tennis. Both sports employ the same muscles a goaltender uses, and, I believe, in the same way.

No other position is so lonely, so chock full of pressure, and so rewarding. The tension created when you face a forward sweeping in is exhilarating. Some goalies feel that pressure as fun. Ron Hextall's musical goalposts routine keeps him fired up and fiercely competitive. Others get ulcers. Montreal greats Bill Durnan and Gerry McNeil both left the game before their time for that reason. Terry Sawchuk was a nervous, twitching, hawk-like man, but virtually invincible in his prime. Glenn Hall, nicknamed "Mr Goalie," had a queasy stomach and more than once left the ice suddenly during a stoppage in play, returning, without explanation, a few minutes later.

Often, while asleep on an airplane, Hall would kick a leg out into the aisle, making the save, even in his sleep.

Goaltending is a game all by itself, a craft in opposition to the activity of every other player on the ice. A goalkeeper must have and maintain confidence at all times, but the goalie who endures must go beyond mere confidence and play without fear. Even though I used a face cage, I had my eyeglasses smashed at least once a year, yet I never thought about it, never worried that it might happen again. Risk is one of the attractions of the game for all the players; the goalie's position is the riskiest of all, and so he is the one that must play beyond fear, in a state of pure concentration.

If a goalie has been injured by a shot to the head, the opposition — and even his teammates in practise — will test his nerve by cranking a few slapshots at eye level. Any sign that the goalie is puck-shy will get him shipped to the minor leagues. The management explains that the goalie is ''playing his way back into shape.'' The players know the real reason.

A goalie's exterior equipment is no less peculiar and individualistic than his mental equipment. Besides the mask there is the stick, the glove, the blocker, and the protective pads — all outsized, flamboyant, totally unlike the other players' gear.

A good pair of friendly pads are vital. Playing at 190 pounds, I always wore light ones, and worked a new pair in during practise so that they would have enough give to prevent rebounds in a game. All goalies soon learn that the most vulnerable space they guard lies between their legs. In the inventive lexicon of the netminder, this area is known as ''the shed'' or ''the five hole.'' Once those pads open, it takes time to close them again. One of the tricks of the trade is to give opposing forwards a glimpse at this opening before closing the pads. This strategy is known as ''the give and take.'' It is seldom talked about, yet all goalies use it, at whatever level of play. It's a way of thinking, a war of wits between the goalie and the man with the puck. ''I gave him the top right hand corner and I expected him to take it. Then I took it away.''

I used to pretend I wasn't aware of the space I'd created between my legs, or between my leg and the nearest post, or how much wide-open net I was giving on the glove side. A forward, seeing that gaping hole or open twine, turned saucer-eyed and fired for the opening. One of the finest saves of my short career occurred when I left six inches or so between my right leg and the post. It was a tiny opening but it was there, established, given. The guy bearing down on me was one of the best sharpshooters in the league, a superb natural goalscorer who had the intelligence and the imagination to want to make such a shot. If it had been anyone else on the ice coming in on that breakaway, I would have given a more obvious and larger space. I saw his eyes shift to the open corner — I always watched the forward's eyes and then, and only then, the puck. He fired a wicked drive, about two inches off the ice and perfectly placed. I didn't wait to find out where the shot was going. It wouldn't have done me any good to know, because he was in so close, I was at his mercy. The puck caromed off my turned out skate and ricocheted up over the glass into the crowd. The crowd gasped, then let out a roar. He skated around the back of the net, shaking his head in disbelief. My teammates all came back to congratulate me, but I paid no attention to their praise. The opposing sniper swung out in front of my crease, pivoted in front of me, and said: ''How did you do that? That's the greatest save I've ever seen.''

If he'd said that I'd been lucky or it was a fluke, I'd have ignored him. To this day I cherish his comment, and have always considered it to be one of the finest compliments I've received. But deep down, behind my shrug and modest smile, I knew I had only "read the play" and practised my craft, the art of goalkeeping.

In addition, I became adroit at deflecting sure goals high on the stick side with a huge wad of black tape fixed to the knob of my goalie stick. "High on the stick side" is a major weakness for young goalies, so I practised deflecting shots by aiming my wad of tape at flying pucks destined for the upper left hand corner. It was little different from redirecting a shot off my pads, or steering a drive to the corner with my stick. After a save like this, opposing forwards often cried "What a fluke!" as they wheeled away from the net. I knew better. When it happened two or three times in the same game, so did they.

Saves like these happen in nearly every game in the NHL, where the goaltenders keep mental books on the scoring habits of the opposition forwards. But such saves bring no less satisfaction to the hard-bitten pro than they do to the minor league netminder playing before a few hundred hometown fans. For a goalie, any goalie, there is no greater satisfaction.

In building a goalie, we've put in a unique personality and we've added the peculiar gear. What's still needed are the skills — skills like the poke-check and the sweep check, two vital moves in any goaltender's repertoire. Knowing when to hold back and wait to poke-check the puck off an opponent's stick takes near-perfect timing. The sweep check is particularly effective in dealing with forwards moving out from behind the net. As well, a goalie must become proficient in knocking down centering passes coming from behind the net. Forwards are in the habit of attempting to flip the puck out in front of the net. A good glove and a whacking good stick discourage this practise. I loved wearing my favourite first baseman's trapper as a hockey glove, with a sponge and tight-fitting glove worn on the inside for added protection. The familiarity of this glove, which I wore virtually the year round as season over-lapped season, was a distinct advantage in both hockey and baseball.

A good goaltender like Billy Smith must constantly challenge the forwards: he must know them and be aggressive with them — within his domain. I never let anyone anywhere near my crease, and hacked at them if they got too close, for those transgressors were violating one of the unwritten laws of the game: you do not disturb or mess with the other team's goalie. When Tiger Williams first began crashing into goal-tenders, I was appalled, for it signaled a change in the un-written etiquette of the game. And now some goaltenders are retaliating, and the results are getting ugly. Sylvain Turgeon was forced to miss the '87 Canada Cup after Ron Hextall broke his forearm during a practise session.

Once, when I was playing in a local playoff game, the opposing team's leading goalscorer sped after a loose puck at our blueline. With no defenceman in sight, I took off in a race for the puck. When we were 10 feet away, it was clear it was going to be a photo-finish. I shouted "Go high!" as I hit the ice, sliding the puck into my pads. He went high, his stick still trying to make a play and free the puck as his skates floated over my face. The play whistled down for a face-off; there was no need to discuss the play with each other. But we both knew "the game had been played," and the gentleman's code of conduct had been observed, as it had to be, at least in those days.

Canadian Amateur Hockey Association coaches are advised to ask, among others, these two questions in choosing a goaltender: Does he give up easy? Does he work hard during practises?

Any goaltender who's made it to the top will tell you that a positive response to the first question is vital, and that the second question is nonsense, and could only be asked by someone who has never played nets. A goaltender faces too many shots a year during games as it is; to ''put out'' during practise, when teammates are coming in on you from all sides, to stay alert for shots that have no meaning, no importance — this is impossible. In fact, a goalie will quickly burn out if he tries to play every shot as if the Stanley Cup hung in the balance. Forwards delight in antagonizing a goaltender during practise. They come in too close, and blast away at will. This may be good for their collective egos, but it is never good for the goalie. It has little to do with situations that occur during a game. (I never cared how many goals were scored on me during practise. When my teammates used me for target practise from time to time, I'd skate out of the net and go for a stroll, returning only when they agreed to stop.) The goalie must have time to follow the flight of the puck into his glove. And he must have time to get set up for the next shot. Otherwise, the practise is of little use to him.

It is easy to wax philosophical about the role of the netminder. He is the final assimilator, for half the game a witness who only watches, an introvert behind a mask. For the other half of the game, he is an acrobat, a dancer, a magician who draws the spotlight to his side. He is the god behind the mask, a perfectionist. Like a good coach, he takes the blame if the team loses.

He is different from everyone else. Often, in a discreet manner, opposing goalies will signal to each other at the end of a good game. They share a common experience, a particular way of seeing.

So much depends upon a goaltender, but the rewards are great, for it is not only the puck that stops here, it is also time. There are few moments more rewarding in a life of hockey than making an outstanding save on the glove side. In the first game of the Rendez-Vous '87 series against the Soviets, Oiler netminder Grant Fuhr robbed Fetisov of a sure goal from the slot with a brilliant split-save off a wicked drive that left Fuhr on his back, skates in the air, and the puck safely stowed in his outsized trapper. The roar of the crowd and the sprawling Fuhr were seen over and over again on replays and in one's mind. Fuhr's great glove snatches the bullet that knocks him down, and ''he holds on,'' as Danny Gallivan used to shout. And for a split second everything is suspended; time too is held and, after the melee and the tumult, there is simply you and the puck in your glove in a frozen moment in time and there is no feeling like it on earth.

The Boys of Winter

Do you think we have a Mario Lemieux? Do you think we have a Wayne Gretzky?

— former Soviet coach Tarasov

When I told a friend in Montreal that I was writing a book on Canadian hockey, his initial reaction was a warning: "Don't wax romantic about the game!" What he was articulating was the collective failure of our imagination. We suffer by having such a small population, and many of those who live here suffer from frozen imaginations.

As of fall, 1987, on the edge of another interminable NHL season, it comes down to this: Canadians do not wish to have a distinctive national identity.

This indifferent country, that worships mostly money and mediocrity, sees the quest for a national identity as a passing phase, a gently warming wave that comes once a generation, then subsides on the same rocky shore. With the possibility of free trade, we open ourselves even more — if that's possible — to American influence and domination.

The game that for over a century has highlighted the best

183

of the Canadian spirit has fallen victim to the forces that have distorted our entire culture: high finance, big business, television, meaningless violence. These have done their dirty work on the game of hockey, one of our greatest national — even natural — resources.

And yet. And yet, paradoxically, despite this — hockey has survived. Like the country, it has survived. From the tedious goonery and disintegration of the game in the '70s, hockey has re-emerged in the '80s as if risen from the grave.

First there was the 1987 Stanley Cup. The Oilers passed beautifully on the fly, Gretzky & Company employed all of their imaginative skills against never-say-die Philadelphia, and Oilers such as the unsung Kevin Lowe played above and and beyond themselves.

It is ridiculous to think of the Oilers as ''the good guys'' and the Flyers as ''the force of destruction,'' and yet, throughout the country, a collective sigh of relief was heard. The *game* had triumphed, been preserved, even honoured by Edmonton's victory. When I went to the office the following morning, several colleagues shook my hand without a word passing between us. No talk was necessary; all was understood. The good things the game stands for — speed, imagination, talent, skill, finesse — these had emerged victorious. A team from Canada had won the Stanley Cup for the fourth time in the last four years. Perhaps the latter was reason enough to celebrate, though Canadians would be the last to admit it.

The night of September 15, 1987, brought us Team Canada's come-from-behind victory over the Soviets in the Canada Cup and made it clear once again — this time to the world — that our boys of winter could triumph at the game. Team Canada assistant coach Jean Perron warned us to buckle our seat belts ''for a trip into hockey space'' and that's where we went: the final three games displayed a kind of hockey beyond the reach of the NHL. In the end, the 44-day-old Canadian team overcame two three-goal deficits to come out on top. The team won on creativity, toughness, resolve, and pride. And all this against one of the most magnificent teams in the world. For the first time in a long while, the business of hockey was overshadowed by the game. The fierce determination of the Canadian players was best summed up by the gritty Doug Gilmour, who said, "We kept one foot on the edge of the bench so that when somebody put the puck in, we were in a good position to jump over the boards."

The picture of Wayne "The Invisible" cradled in the arms of Mario "The Best" — after the latter scored the winning goal in the second overtime of the second game — did more for English-French relations in this country than a rink-full of Canadian politicians. This extraordinary, emotion-packed final series filled the country with pride. Lemieux's series-winning goal straightened the backbone of the nation.

Ice binds us together, shapes and defines both our style and our substance. It informs us, connects us rink by rink to ourselves. In the Canadian psyche, the motion we create on our national icescape is the nearest we come to permanence.

For Canadians, hockey represents the play of life, with all its inherent paradoxes and contradictions — the boys of winter cavorting in a white transparent world of ritual and make-believe. For good or ill, the way we feel about the game tells us more about ourselves than we'd like to know. The stalwart image of Canadians in the world contrasts with the risk and abandon we bring to the game — risk and abandon that we don't usually allow in our lives. The essence of hockey for Canadians is that it brings together both the imagined world and the real one, both the abstract and the actual, fused. This beautiful game that brings such joy lets us live imaginatively, lets us go beyond the self and reach for the dream so repressed in our high-tech society, where one's own feelings and accomplishments are increasingly pushed beneath ''the bottom line.'' We long to see individual effort, sacrifice, discipline, and team effort ''pay off,'' as it were. These are the human values we intrinsically believe in, and our heroes of hockey act them out for us all. On ice we are transformed. Time itself freezes for an instant, so that you and I can spend a spine-chilling night or two each week out on the shining pond (even if we're only in front of our TVs).

All that has happened to hockey in the last few decades has done little to change the feeling of the Canadian — boy or girl, man or woman, of 7, 17 or 70 — who steps out on the ice.

Bibliography

Abel, Allan. *But I Loved It Plenty Well*. Toronto, Collins. 1983.

Bergler, Edmund Dr. *The Battle of the Conscience*. Washington. Washington Institute of Medicine. 1948.

Berton, Pierre. *Vimy*. Toronto. McClelland & Stewart. 1986.

Camus, Albert. *Notebooks*. New York. Knopf. 1965.

Camus, Albert. *Lyrical and Critical Essays*. New York. Knopf. 1968.

Cutler, Michael. *hockey masks*. Montreal. Tundra Books. 1977.

Dryden, Ken. *The Game*. Toronto. Macmillan. 1983.

Dryden, Ken and Mark Mulvoy. *Face-Off At The Summit*. Toronto, Little-Brown. 1973.

Duhatschek, Eric and Steve Simmons. *On Fire*. Winlaw, B.C. Polestar Press. 1986.

Eskenazi, Gerald. *A Thinking Man's Guide to Pro Hockey*. New York. Doubleday. 1972, revised 1976.

Fischler, Stan. *All-Time Hockey Trivia Book*. New York. National Sports Publishing Corporation. 1979.

Franz, Marie Louise. *On Divination and Synchronicity*. Toronto. Summer City Books. 1980.

Goyens, Chrys and Allan Turowetz. *Lions in Winter*. Scarborough, Ontario. Prentice-Hall. 1986.

Graves, Robert. *Goodbye To All That*.

Gzowski, Peter. *The Game Of Our Lives*. Toronto. McClelland and Stewart. 1981.

Hannah, Barbara. *Active Imagination.* Santa Monica, California. Sigo Press. 1981.

Hewitt, Foster. *Hockey Night in Canada.* Toronto. Ryerson Press. 1953.

Hood, Hugh. *Strength Down Centre: The Jean Beliveau Story.* Scarborough. Prentice-Hall. 1970.

Hood, Hugh. *The Governor's Bridge Is Closed.* ''The Pleasures of Hockey'' in Ottawa. Oberon. 1973.

Hood, Hugh. *Scoring: the art of hockey.* Ottawa. Oberon. 1979.

Imlach, Punch. *Hockey Is A Battle.* Toronto. Macmillan. 1969.

Kidd, Bruce and John Macfarlane. *The Death of Hockey.* Toronto. New Press. 1972.

Kroker, Arthur. *Technology and the Canadian Mind.* Montreal. New World Perspectives. 1984.

Lessing, Doris. *Briefing For a Descent Into Hell.* New York. Knopf. 1971.

Ludwig, Jack. *Games of Fear and Winning.* Toronto. Doubleday. 1976.

MacGregor, Roy. *The Last Season.* Toronto. Macmillan. 1983.

Maltz, Maxwell Dr. *Psycho-Cybernetics.* Richmond Hill, Ontario. Simon & Schuster. 1969.

McPhee, John. *A Sense of Where You Are.* New York. Farrar, Strauss and Giroux. 1965.

Plimpton, George. *Open Net.* New York. Norton & Company. 1985.

Purdy, Al. *Collected Poems.* Toronto. McClelland & Stewart. 1986.

Ronberg, Gary. *The Hockey Encyclopedia.* New York. Macmillan. 1974.

Sanderson, Derek. *I've Got To Be Me.* New York. Dell. 1970.

Schultz, Dave. *The Hammer: Confessions of a Hockey Enforcer.* Toronto. Totem Books. 1981.

Stephenson, John. *Death, Grief, and Mourning.* New York. Free Press. 1985.

Whitehead, Eric. *Cyclone Taylor: A Hockey Legend.* Toronto. Doubleday. 1977.

Whitehead, Eric. *The Patricks.* Toronto. Doubleday. 1980.

Whitmont, Edward. *Return of the Goddess.* New York. Crossroads. 1984.

Williams, Dave. *Tiger: A Hockey Story.* Vancouver. Douglas & McIntyre. 1984.